TENURIAL CONDITIONS AND MODE OF EXPLOITATION

P.K. Das

RAJAT PUBLICATIONS
New Delhi

Tenurial Conditions and Mode of Exploitation
by *P.K. Das*

This edition is published by Rajat Publications
4740/23, Ansari Road Daryaganj,
New Delhi - 110002

ISBN: 978-81-7880-009-7

Edition 2025

Printed and bound in India

RAJAT
PUBLICATIONS

4740/23, Ansari Road, Daryaganj,
New Delhi- 110002 (India)
Mob:- +91-9811484973, +91-9811105389
E-mail: rajat_publication@yahoo.com

Dedicated to
My Parents
Guruji Biswanath Das
and
Smt. Kokila Das

PREFACE

Discussions concerning tenancy and its economic effects date back to early tracts in economic writings wherein debates were carried on as to whether the Metayer system of share-cropping, as developed in France, was inimical to the advancement of agriculture and to the interest of the tenants and / or landlords. The issues have been revived, in recent times, in context of land reforms and the transitions in agricultural production conditions. Questions raised concern, among others, the relative efficiency of owner operated, tenanted and capitalist farms as well as comparative performance of different tenurial systems (mainly share-cropping and fixed rent). These comparisons are made in terms of static efficiency measured as net income generated per unit of land and also in relation to possibilities of investment or adoption of technical changes promoting productivity. Differences in conclusion mainly arise from those assumptions as to who takes decisions, what are the decision making variables and the particular constraints within which they operate. The various models are constructed in the context of stylised situations either in terms of competitive market or with some marginal modifications of the same. These theoretical discussions have either failed to take account of the particular way in which the agrarian markets, given the historically developed property relations, function or the assumptions have been too restrictive and therefore, cannot be easily generalised. Empirical information on tenancy, too, has often been gathered rather incidentally, the main focus being on other aspects more commonly technological relations. Or for lack of analytical framework, the information collected, although detailed, is often piecemeal and hence in a form that can throw meagre light on tenurial conditions and their economic consequences. An attempt has been made here to focus on certain aspects of tenancy question which have been inadequately considered if not totally missed out in both model building exercise as well as data collection. Information thought to be crucial for analysing the question of tenancy, to understand the functioning of the lease market and mode of exploitation with possible variations that accompany the leases were collected through survey of eleven villages spread over different parts of Orissa at two different points of time — first during 1974-75 and the second in 1991-92 with a view to see the transition in tenancy situation. On the basis of these information, certain features of the lease market have been discussed — who leases out to whom and who leases in from whom; the various motivational forces that influence each lease and lease terms and conditions; in what sizes the land parcels are to be leased out in what form the rent is to be collected — kind rent, fixed cash rent or on crop sharing basis. Data collected from these villages reveal the prevalence of different modes of exploitation among irrigated, unirrigated, tribal and cash crop producing areas. Following the introduction of irrigation and cultivation of high yielding variety of paddy a complete shift has been observed — from share-cropping to fixed kind rent, then to fixed cash rent and finally to fixed cash rent paid in advance. Landlords are able to extract more or secure less depending upon their relative resource strength compared to that of tenants to whom they lease out. Generally, the dominant party in the land-lease market exploits the weaker party participating in the process of leasing in or leasing out. The situation worsens when the weaker party is left with no choice but to enter into the market for his mere survival and when the dominant party combines multiple functions enjoying power in a number of markets simultaneously, the weaker party is subjected to further exploitation through various price and non-price channels. If the landlord is a merchant he may exploit the weak position of the tenant cultivator in the lease market and make the lease conditional upon the tenant producing certain stipulated crops and selling them to him. If the landlord combines the function of usury the tenant farmer may lose the freedom of taking decisions (as to what to produce) and may also be asked unpaid or underpaid labour services and if the tenant farmer is unable to repay the loan (which is very likely because of weak economic position of the tenant) he remains perpetually indebted to the lessor who may require him to pledge his and sometimes even his family's future labour. In view of the situation of interlocked markets and its dynamic effects, the dominant parties seem to enhance their exploitative hold by linking up several transactions directly.

The relative resource strength of the lessor vis-a-vis his lessees appears to influence the rent per acre under fixed kind and cash system. Generally, the smaller tenants pay a higher rent per acre than the bigger ones. The productivity per acre is generally higher in case of small tenants. In most cases the leases are accompanied by some amount of hidden labour rent. The fixed cash rent system prevailed in two widely different sets of economic circumstances — first where the economically depressed "landlords" lease out under financial difficulties for fixed cash rent even if it turns out to be lower than the money equivalent of fixed kind rent or the actual crop share. Fixed cash system of rent payment prevails widely replacing the conventional share-cropping and fixed kind system of rent payment. The lease periods have been conspicuously shortened increasing the insecurity of the tenants and with every renewal/fresh lease the rent is enhanced.

I had the unique opportunity to work under the supervision of Late Professor Krishna Bharadwaj of Jawaharlal Nehru University, New Delhi without whose academic support and advice this work would not have been possible. I feel privileged and honoured to have been associated with a scholar of such eminence and I owe a deep sense of gratitute to her.

I am also indebted to my brother Professor G.K.Das formerly Director, South Campus, University of Delhi and formerly Vice-Chancellor, Utkal University, Bhubaneswar, whose persistent pressure initiated me into the field of research. I express my deep gratitude to him with all humility.

What I have done would not have been possible without the unqualified support of my family and their loving encouragement. Elli, my wife, shouldered the entire responsibility of taking care of the children and domestic chores making me free to pursue my studies. My son Bapi, daughter-in-law-Pooja, daughter Chumki and son-in-law Akash had been insisting on completing this work. Finally after a long gap this work could see the light of the day. I am thankful to Ms Rashma Zaidi for designing this cover outlook. I am greatly indebted to Shri. R.N. Bhardwaj for helping me in editing and to Smt. Bimla Bhardwaj for her help in proof reading.

Finally, I thank my publisher M/s. Rajat Publications, New Delhi, for the hardship they took in going through the manuscript and bringing out this publication.

P. K. Das

CONTENTS

1

SOME ANALYTICAL IMPLICATIONS

Debates on tenurial systems and agrarian relation and comparative performances of share-cropping, ownership and capitalist system of farming are much in vogue in the context of the adoption of land reform measures in different countries. In fact, the discussions on the relative efficiency of resource allocation in cropsharing and ownership farming can be traced back to the classical writings in political economy.

Writing on the comparative inefficiency of the "Metayage system", Adam Smith was of the opinion that Metayers (believed to be successors of the slave cultivators of the farmers). Tenants "are least interested to lay out in the further improvement of the land, any part of the little stock which they might save from their own share of the produce because the lord who laid out nothing was to get one half of whatever is produced."[1] A full proprietory right to the peasant farmer would provide him with an incentive for intensive land use applying more of labour and non-labour resources and increase agricultural production. Comparing the tenant farmer with the peasant proprietors Smith says that it is like a "merchant who trades with borrowed money compared with one who trades with his own. The stock of both may improve, but that of the one with equal good conduct must always improve more slowly than that of the other on account of the large share of the profits which is consumed by the interest of the loan. The land cultivated by the farmer must in the same manner, with only equal good conduct, be improved more slowly than those cultivated by the proprietor, on account of the large share of the produce which is consumed in the rent and which had the farmer been the proprietor he might have employed in the further improvement of the land. The status of a farmer besides is, from the nature of things inferior to that of proprietor."[2]

The tenant farmer pays the land rent which is considered as "the price paid for the use of land is naturally the highest which the tenant can afford to pay in the actual circumstances of the land. In adjusting, the terms of lease the landlord endeavours to give him no greater share of the produce than what is sufficient to keep up the stock from which he furnishes seed, pays the labour, and purchases and maintains the cattle and other instruments of husbandry."[3] This is evidently the smallest share with which the tenant can content himself. "The landlord demands rent even for the unimproved land, when lease come to be renewed, however, the landlord commonly demands the same augmentation of rent as if they have been all made of the his own."[4] Rent is therefore, not at all proportionate to the improvements made by the landlord but is like a monopoly price, and the landlord tries to squeeze the tenant to the maximum and therefore, under a Metayage system of land cultivation, the tenant is left with so little of the total produce that he loses all interest to improve the productivity of land or make any intensive use of land. Smith thus concludes that such a system of agricultural production is inefficient compared to the peasant farming, and therefore, should be condemned.

But in few cases, Smith writes on to say, that the farmer might sometimes be "interested to lay out part of their capital in the further improvement of the farm; because they may sometimes expect to recover it with a large profit before the expiration of the lease."[5] But such a thing will occur only under the assumption to tenurial security that is, the lease should be given for a specific period of time; such a security of tenure will induce a farmer to "engage only in those improvements whose effects will last no longer than lease period, unless the lease is long enough to allow the profit arising from his improvements to repay the whole outlay together with the interest. It is in this way that long leases operate to increase the product of the land... the farmers' certainty of reaping the advantage till the end of his lease, is equally conducive to the improvements of the landed property with the length of the leases."[6] Insecurity of land tenure therefore, stands in the way of improvement of land.

Thus, Smith denounces the Metayage system of land cultivation and he says that the system is inefficient compared to peasant farming. Smith's views have also been supported by Arthur Young, who says that land under a Metayage system is most miserably cultivated and thus he condemns the system of letting out land. Under such a system the landlord enjoys the major proportion of the produce and the tenant is left with only the bare minimum hardly giving him any incentive to increase production.

Like Smith, Alfred Marshall also condemns the share-cropping system of land cultivation. In such a system, Marshall argues, the landlord is but a sleeping partner and appropriates a major share of the gross produce of the leased out land as rent. This apart, the landlords have generally "included the right to claim certain labour services, dues, tolls and presents and the amount he obtained under each of these heads varied from time to time; from place to place and from one landlord to another... the landlord was likely to use his superior strength to raise payments in some from or other."[7] Usually, the tenant is left with a very little of the total produce after paying the rent to the landlord and consequently the tenant's capacity to invest further in agriculture is reduced to minimum. The incentive to invest in cultivation of the leased in land is reduced due to the fact that "the cultivator has to give to his landlord half of the returns to each dose of capital and labour that he applies to land it will not be to his interest to apply any dose the total return to which is less than twice enough to reward himself, so that the landlord will get a smaller share even if those returns than he would have on the plan of a fixed payment".[8] Compared to this Marshall writes on to say, that farming under a peasant proprietor will be more efficient since the peasant farmer enjoys more freedom of choice of inputs and crop production.

Thus, the classical and neoclassical view is that tenant farms are less efficient than owner cultivated ones. The Metayer system of share-cropping developed in France was inimical to the growth of agricultural production and to the interests of tenant farmers and landlord. Assuming that the size of lease holding and the tenant's share as a proportion of output fixed and all costs of cultivation being borne by the tenant the classical and neoclassical economists view that tenant cultivated farms are necessarily less efficients than owner operated ones. A tenant will be less induced to invest in land because of the fact that the fruits of his investment will accrue more to the landlord than to himself. Therefore, the classical view is that the tenant would put in less of inputs in the cultivation of the leased in land since returns to him is only a part of the total produce. While the classical viewed the cropsharing tenancy to be inefficient in the long term sense i.e. in terms of productive investment and growth potential the neoclassicals were concerned more with the static question of current productivity of land. In case of the tenant operated farms the marginal return curve of inputs for the tenant is proportionately lower all through than in the case of owner cultivated farms, facing the same production function. Hence, the equilibrium level of output for the same farm is lower in the former case. Thus, land is used less intensively in the case of tenant cultivated farms, leading to a lower level of output.

The incentive to invest (even in current inputs) thus may suffer under the tenurial system of crop cultivation since neither the landlord nor the tenant can appropriate the full returns to the investments made. Further, the situation is worsened (particularly, for long term investments) by tenurial insecurity since leases are either temporary or terminable at any time. On the part of the landlord, the possibility of misuse and careless utilisation of land by the tenant is suggested as a reason for short leases.

Contrary to the tenant's position, an owner cultivator has many advantages. "He is free to do what he likes, he is not worried by the interference of a landlord and the anxiety lest another should reap the fruits of his work and self denial. His feeling of ownership gives him self respect, and stability of character and makes him provident and temperate in his habits. He is scarcely ever ideal and seldom regards his work as mere drudgery, it is all for the land he loves so well."[9]

To sum up, "there is not a single word," as Arthur Young points out, "to be said in favour of the practice and a thousand arguments that might be used against it. In this most miserable of all the modes of letting land, the defrauded landlord receives a contemptible rent; the farmer is in the lowest state of poverty; the land is miserably cultivated and the nation suffers as severely as the parties themselves... whatever the system prevails it may be taken for granted that a useless and miserable population is found."[10]

We find a number of contemporary writings in economics supporting the views of the classical and neoclassical economics. Similar to the classical view that sharecropping will be less efficient, Charles Isswai holds the view that "other things being equal, inputs will be greater under a system of fixed rent than under one where costs are borne by the tenant and the gross produce is shared in any proportion by tenant or landlord."[11] In other words, he says that "under a system of fixed rents output will be greater and investment is more likely to take place than under a system in which the landlord shares the crop with the tenant whatever the ratio of cropsharing and whatever the size of rent. It is needless to say this ratio and the size of the rent have very important indirect effects on the farmer's willingness and ability to improve and invest as well as on his welfare. No less important is the security of tenure enjoyed by the tenant."[12] Fixed rent, in short, has a favourable effect on productivity where as a share-cropping arrangement of land lease has an adverse effect on productivity and on investment as well.[13]

Similar views have also been expressed by De Gale Johnson who says, that "under a cropshare lease, if the landlord's share of the crops is half the tenant will apply his resources in production of crops until the marginal cost of crop output is equal to half the value of the marginal output."[14] Insecurity of the lease discourages the tenant cultivator to invest in land since the tenant cultivator is doubtful of appropriating the fruits of the investment at all. Therefore, it will further reduce the efficiency of the cropsharing leases.

"One of the most important economic arguments for land reform arises," John W. Mellor writes, "from the tendency for landlord — tenant arrangements to discourage production — increasing innovation because they do not allow a sufficient proportion of the gains of innovation to accrue to the cultivator."[15]

The landlord tries to "bleed all income from the tenant" beyond the necessaries of life either through enhancing the rent in some form or other whenever there is an evidence of increased income. Such a system therefore, would not provide any incentive to income increasing innovation by tenants. Share-rental system (when costs are shared by the landlord and the tenant) may be less pernicious, but still greatly discourages production. Michael Lipton also observes, "a secured tenant agriculture without share-cropping, and with adequate access to credit, is much less unequal, less exploitative and less inefficient than existing cropshare system."[16]

Under the share-cropping lease system A.K. Sen using his concept of real, labour cost, argues, that resource allocation would be inefficient no matter whether it is the gross output or net output which is shared between the landlord and the tenant. In case of the latter, when net output is shared, "since (h) ['h' is the share of the produce obtained by the sharecropper] is less than 1, the share-cropper's relevant labour cost is higher than the real labour cost. Output will thus be restricted and marginal product of labour will exceed the real cost of labour. There is thus misallocation under share-cropping... In the case of sharing, the gross output the misallocation is more pervasive. When the gross output is shared the non-labour factor will not be allocated according to the proper marginal cost and products and this will create allocative distortions even if the labour application formula is the same as under peasant farming."[17] Sen thus concludes that quite apart from the problem of 'equity' and 'exploitation' involved in sharecropping, there is also a problem of inefficient allocation.

The opinion of classical and neoclassical economists that sharecropping system of land lease results in inefficient allocation of resources has been challenged by S.N.S. Cheung.[18] Cheung's contention is that, share tenancy is a land lease under which the rent paid by the tenant is a contracted percentage of the output yield per period of time. As a rule the landlord provides the land and the tenant provides the labour, other inputs may be provided by either party. "Share tenancy is thus share contracting defined here as two or more individual parties combining privately owned resources for the production of certain mutually agreed outputs, the actual outputs to be shared according to certain mutually accepted percentages as returns to the contracting parties for their productive resources forsaken. The theory to be derived from standard economic principles may be generalised to all forms of land tenure under similar ownership of resources."[19] Cheung argues that this traditional inefficiency argument is illusory and writes on to say that allocation of resources in the crop production will remain unaffected disregarding the fact whether the land is under self-cultivation or leased out on cropsharing system or fixed rent paid either in kind or cash. "In other words, different contractual arrangements do not imply different efficiencies of resource use as long as these arrangements are themselves aspects of private property rights."[20] Under share contracts the tenant will continue to stay in farming so long as the marginal productivity of land is greater than zero with all farming inputs other than land held constant. To maximise wealth the landowner will raise the rental percentage until the tenant's income from farming equals his alternative earning.

In the case of fixed rent the implied resource use will not change. Under a fixed rent system the tenant independently decides the amount of land and non-land resources to be invested in the leased in land, while under a share-cropping lease the tenant and the landowner mutually decide the intensity of non-land inputs. " In either case, the wealth maximising value determines the land size per farm as well as other inputs employed... Since, the set of constraints for the decision making is the same for the two types of contracts, the same resource is implied... Thus under fixed rent, the land size per farm and the rental annuity received by the landowner will be exactly the same as under share tenancy."[21]

Cheung further argues that duration of land lease contracts does not have any adverse effect on productivity. He contends that arguments commonly used in support of the alleged inefficiency of lease duration of less than ten years are not true. Tenurial insecurity being high in case of short lease duration, the tenants are less induced to invest. But this opinion has been challenged by Cheung, who views that such a conclusion is untrue, since there has been "no evidence to show that in China productivity under tenancy varies with the duration of the lease contract."[22]

Thus, Chenug refutes the traditional views of inefficient use of resource allocation under share tenancy and holds the opinion that "different contractual arrangements do not imply different efficiencies of resource allocation as long as property rights are exclusive and transferable."[23]

Cheung's model operates in a perfectly competitive set up and competition for resource ownership will induce efficient contracts where both parties, the landlord and tenants, will try to adjust the resources so that they are most efficiently utilised.

Thus, within a competitive framework, where all resources are rewarded at competitive rates and hence implicitly under full employment conditions, Cheung argues, that there is parity among all systems of farming, whether peasant farming, share-cropping tenancy, fixed rent tenancy or capitalist farming.

Conclusions almost similar to this have been arrived at by Chakravarty and Rudra. Their study being based on the data from the Farm Management Studies goes on to conclude, that "there are not very many marked differences in the input-output patterns of owner operated farms and tenant operated farms." [24] Subsequently another study, by Dwivedy and Rudra [25] goes on to confirm this view point that productive efficiency is invariant as between different system of cultivation. Another study by Nirmal Chandra also suggests that tenancy is not significantly related to output per acre as the labour in put per acre. However, the reasons for their (Rudra and Chandra) conclusions we believe are very different from those of Cheung and their results cannot be interpreted as supporting Cheung's position.

Cheung's assumptions are far from supported by the prevailing conditions in an economy particularly where the wage employment opportunities are highly discontinuous and uncertain and the distribution of land ownership is highly inequitous. "The competitive assumptions are violated in a fundamental way in an economy in which the extent of market penetration, as also the character of markets, is very different... The extent and type of involvements in the market of the different sections of the peasantry are not at all uniform."[26] For a detailed discussion of the qualitatively different characteristics of rural markets and market involvement of different sections of peasantry we may refer here to Krishna Bharadwaj's study "Production Conditions in Indian Agriculture."

Commenting on the conclusions of Cheung, Bardhan and Srinivasan argue that, increase in production uncertainty induces the tenant and the "landlord to go in opposite directions in the market for land leases. Contradicting certain views of Cheung these authors hold the opinion that Cheung's conclusion of inefficient allocation of resources under share-cropping tenancy is wrong does not seem to hold true in a situation where a share-cropper will not use as much of variable factor (in this case the labour) as an owner farmer would."[27]

Further these authors have also disagreed with Cheung's proposition — that the percentage shares and area rented under tenancy are competitively determined in the land lease market. In his analysis Cheung himself contends that rent is determined by the landlord himself, where as in a competitive market rent should be accepted as given or determined by the large number of tenants and landlord as well.[28] There is a continuing controversy over the specific assumptions of the Bardhan-Srinivasan model and its approach to the tenancy problem which we refrain from detailing here.[29]

The above models have been worked out to compare the efficiency (or inefficiency) of the owner operated, tenant operated either on fixed or cropsharing arrangements, or capitalist basis. These studies have been based on certain assumptions highlighting only partially a particular aspect of the tenancy question. The various models have been constructed in the context of stylised situations, either in terms of competitive markets or with some marginal modifications of the same. What is missing is the significance of certain historical factors which, through property relations pertaining to the agrarian situation under consideration, influence the nature and the functioning of markets themselves.[30]

The initial economic resource position of the tenant

vis-a-vis the landlord largely influences the production conditions in which the particular tenant is to function. The economic status of cultivating household, no matter whether peasant operated, tenant operated, or if a capitalist farm, largely influences the land utilisation, the cropping pattern, the level of employment and so on.[31] The relative bargaining strength (reinforced by forces of tradition, custom and social mores) determines the access to resources, the terms on which they can be obtained and the fields of feasible choices open to the individual producer in the various markets, or in short his current production activities and his income and asset position resulting therefrom.[32]

In an economy where employment opportunities are highly uncertain, the farms (whether tenant operated or owner cultivated) largely based on the family labour are likely to have higher intensity of cultivation than a capitalist farm based on employing wage labour. Whilst the capitalist farms stop employing further wage labour in their farms after the point where the marginal product of labour equals the prevailing wage rate, the farms using family labour will extend cultivation beyond this point. The tenant operated farms may suggest theoretically less intensive use of various productive resources, largely the non-labour resources. However, this need not be so necessarily. It would depend upon the objective functions attributable to the tenant and owner cultivators. Moreover, the objective function itself is not to be attributed in any *a priori* fashion as economists have tended to do. The objective depends itself upon the resource position and hence the economic status of the particular cultivating household. The small owner and tenant farmers would try to use their operational (land) holding more intensively in order to raise a subsistence for their mere survival. This may so happen because income outside the farm are quite uncertain and meagre. In such a case we may not find a noticeable difference in the owner operated and tenant cultivated farms and the tenant operated farms may operate beyond the competitive equilibrium point.[33] Such a situation may also increase the exploitative hold of the landlord who tries to extract more from the tenant and capitalise the gains of increase in production.[34]

This can be visualised better when we study the initial resource position of the tenant, owner cultivators, capitalist farmers or large landlords (lessors), in relation to the markets like employment, credit and so on. In a situation, where the large landowner with high social and economic status quite often combines multiple functions, he consequently enjoys a dominant position in a number of markets simultaneously. Such a situation allows a superior position to the landlord and enables him to exploit the tenant in various forms. Where the landlord combines the function of a lessor and a trader or a money lender he enjoys the advantage of stipulating crop production or the sale of crops i.e. to whom to sell and at what price etc. Thus, the tenant's choice of crop may be constrained. The landlord with his superior position may demand exorbitant rents or may demand from the tenant unpaid or under paid labour services to be rendered to the landlord in various forms. The exploitative power of the superior party in the contract, here the lessor, enhances because he is operating in more than one market. For example in a situation of semi-feudal character, where the tenant is bound to the landlord through consumption loans the landlord combines in himself the functions of a rentier and a creditor and may try to maximise his income derived from the twin sources — rent and interest.[35]

Such interpenetration of markets not only increases the exploitative powers of the landlord but also has certain dynamic consequences. The freedom to take decisions or the area of feasible choices for the economically vulnerable sections shrinks and this may, overtime, mean the perpetuation of bondage. Superficially, there are free markets and free choice but in practice the area of feasible choices is limited or can even be non-existent. In the case of a tenant, who has to commit his labour to the landlord, the position may be virtually one of an attached labourer. Further such a situation where in lease and labour are tied up, may have an effect at the macro level on the labour market itself. The landlord's relying upon committed labour of the tenant would inhibit the expansion of wage employment itself in the rural economy and thus the situation would come back to square one, where there is a high premium placed upon leasing-in land, with all the concommittant conditions which limit the tenant's freedom.

The above is a very general description of certain characteristics of rural markets. As to how particular markets do get interlinked and what pattern of exploitation develops in any particular region is a matter of historical development of the particular rural economy under consideration. Two analytical consequences relevant to the present question of tenurial conditions follow : (i) If indeed, markets are interlocked, then it may not be possible to single out or isolate tenancy as the mode of exploitation. The exploitation in the system may not be identifiable by isolating the lease market and depicting the situation as a landlord versus his tenant but rather the economically powerful versus the economically weaker sections of the peasantry. (ii) The initial historical situation relating to property relations and the way market power has developed and is being exercised by the more powerful sections in the rural economy, determine who is taking the decisions concerning the lease, what terms and conditions are attached to it and what choice area is left, if at all, to the weaker party in the deal.

All the different models, while discussing the comparative efficiency of the different forms of cultivation, have attempted to focus on particular aspects of tenancy in the context of stylised situations. But most of these studies analysing the question of tenancy or agrarian relations have been inadequate since these have failed to take account of the particular ways the agrarian markets function or have been based on informations reflecting only partially the question of tenancy. Where such conjoint exploitation exists the actual functioning of the lease market cannot be studied in isolation.

Here, we shall try to concretise the two points rather abstractly expressed above in the context of the villages in Orissa we surveyed. To take up the first point — namely, that the lease market cannot be isolated to understand the play of economic power. The picture of the exploitative landlord may in fact be an overwhelming face of the rural society and in the prevalent power structure, ownership of land may bestow social power on the owner more than proportionately to his financial position. But it is not so much the fact of a landlord versus his tenant, but of the economically powerful versus the economically weak. As we shall see as to who get included in the class of 'landlords' (or 'tenants') is dependent upon a number of historical factors: our villages, belonging mainly to the *Zamindari* belt, had a number of non-cultivating castes declared themselves as 'traditionally landlords'. So also did the terms and conditions vary even within the conventional sharecropping system, depending upon the relative status of the lessor and lessee. In fact in the tribal area, many landlords were small land owners who had become labourers, leasing out their land to relatively better-off tenants. Thus a crucial piece of information relates to *who leases from whom*.

This perhaps explains why some recent empirical studies based on isolating the factor of tenancy as such for studying economic performance come up with negative conclusions. A classification of tenants on the basis of proportion of area leased in to area cultivated thus puts together heterogeneous types of tenants of different status, leasing in land from landlords of varying status on different terms. As we shall note the terms and conditions of leases do show variations among different sets of lessors and lessees.

However, this is not to argue that in the system of exploitation, tenancy is a non-factor. This brings us to our second point. Given the unequal distribution of property and absence of alternative sources of income, the majority of tenants do have no choice but to seek leases and in the prevailing circumstances, the landlords (certainly the big ones) exercise the decision to whom to lease out, in what parcels to lease out and on what terms and conditions. We shall see that the landlord exercises preference for tenants of particular types, depending upon the latter's initial economic resource position. Terms and conditions do very, both according to the relative economic position of the tenant as well as technological situations. Although under the cropsharing system, the share of the major crop may appear to be conventionally fixed, there are many ways by which particular landlords may use the system to extract more (or secure less). Quite often the tenant has to render unpaid or underpaid labour services, the extent and nature of which varies considerably. There can be varying arrangements for sharing of minor crops and by-products; there are various ways in which inputs may be shared, with or without appropriate adjustment in crop shares. Further, there may be shifts in tenurial systems when the technological situation changes as we notice to have happened in some villages where irrigation and high yielding paddy was introduced

The tenurial conditions under any land tenure system should be analysed in relation to the legal, social and economic dimensions of the specific region under study. The importance of this particular factor increases in a situation where we notice the existence of varied legal property relations. The agrarian markets become more complex where exist certain castes of non-cultivating households, who are 'traditionally' landlords, certain sects of people who are similarly cultivating households, and certain castes, generally belonging to the lower strata of the society working as agricultural labourers. These factors influence the lease markets and the employment markets to a large extent. Quite often these factors present themselves as concealed in customs and conventions.

These apart, there are economic factors like the introduction of irrigation, introduction of cash crops which have also great influence on the agrarian markets. Therefore, a study of the landlord-tenant nexus can be more meaningfully conducted if it is analysed in relation to these different factors i.e. who makes the decision and what are the social, legal constraints within which they operate, their position analysed in terms of the relative resource strength of the peasantry. In models of tenancy sometimes, it is hypothesised, that the tenant is the sole decision making entity operating with the constraint of a given size of holding (as in Marshall's model where the tenant provides all the inputs and taxes entirely, takes on his own, the decision of how much to produce); in some others it is left to the landlord who often constrains the output through non-investment. In Cheung's model, the tenant has the free option to work either as a wage labourer or to work on the leased in land and it is through mutual contracting that the crop share and the size for lease parcel get determined. However, the patterns in which economic decisions are shared by the tenant and the landlord can be varying and not always rigidly determined as it is presupposed.

In order to confront, the relative economic status of the lessor and the lessee, ideally speaking, we need a comprehensive index of the total resource position of the two households. Due to lack of comprehensive and reliable information on non-land assets, income from other sources, etc., in the study, we have provisionally taken the size of holding as representing the household's economic strength supplemented by annual net income from all sources. One of the purpose in detailing out who leases from whom is to confront the relative economic status of the landlord and his tenant. While data concerning the size of the holding is relatively easily available that concerning ownership of the other assets, incomes from other sources etc. is rather difficult to obtain. Ideally speaking the economic status should have been represented by a comprehensive index of resource position of individual households. Even this would not be adequate considering that ownership of land may bestow economic status and power beyond the financial value of land owned. To supplement the information on holdings, we have adopted a crude way of calculating the net annual income on the basis of which it may be said that the economic status of the middle class tenants is not much inferior to that of the small landlords. This obviously calls for further refinements.

The particular mode of exploitation conditioned by historical factors reveals itself in the terms and conditions and sizes of leased parcels. In the villages, we studied, the leases, particularly when the tenant was in a weaker position, were accompanied by a clause concerning labour services to be rendered to the landlord. Thus, there was an element of labour rent included in the lease conditions. We have already noted that such a stipulation implies that the tenant ties up his labour, losing freedom to the extent to offer it outside. Further, that tying-up may in turn inhibit the development of wage labour itself. An additional element of hidden labour rent is present in the landlord's leasing-out land in small parcels, and to tenants with large families. Landlord's own explanation for such a preference shows that tenant families would be under pressure to work harder in order to satisfy their minimum needs. With changes in technical conditions, such as introduction of high yielding paddy, we note that the terms and conditions of leases did change. In fact, there was noticeable shift from share-cropping to a fixed rental system of tenancy. However, whether this would bring about fundamental changes in property relations and the mode of exploitation could not be said on the basis of the information we as yet possess. This study, however, is an attempt to explore some of these issues in greater details.

It is presumed that under a cropsharing system the share is conventionally determined. But there exist a number of ways by which any particular landlord may use the system to extract more or secure less. As already mentioned, quite often the tenant may have to render free or underpaid labour services either by working on the self-cultivated plot of the landlord and as a domestic servant. The nature and extent of such services vary considerably. There can be different arrangements with regard to the sharing of by-products, crop shares referring to the main crop, free gifts in terms of fuel wood, money or in kind are not uncommon. There are varying arrangements of sharing of inputs, some landlord may share cost of fertilisers, or pay water charges with or without appropriately adjusting the crop share, where as some do not. Sometimes, a portion of the gross output is set aside before sharing is done, that equals seed requirements advanced by the landlords. There may even be a shift in the tenurial system (as we have seen in one of our sample villages) with changing technical conditions. We have noted that there has been a transition to a fixed rent system form a crop sharing one. The conventional notion that fixed rent is necessarily less exploitative than crop sharing may not be necessarily true. We also find landlords changing the crop sharing arrangements with the introduction of the HYV so as to see that they do not lose their exploitative hold while appropriating simultaneously the gains of HYV cultivation.

Thus, we find that depending upon the initial resource position of the tenant, peasant or capitalist farmer and the socio-economic and historical factors of a particular region, tenurial conditions are determined. The land lease market cannot be studied in isolation since that may lead to misleading conclusions.

REFERENCES

1. Adam Smith, *Wealth of Nations,* Edited by Andrew Skinner (Pelican Classics, 1970), p. 491.
2. *Ibid.*, p. 494.
3. *Ibid.*, p. 247.
4. *Ibid.*, p. 248.
5. *Ibid.*, p. 491.

6. J.B. Say, *A Treaties on Political Economy*. Reprints of Economic Classics (New York, 1964), pp. 366-7.
7. Alfred Marshall, *Principal of Economics*, Eighth Edition (London, 1972), pp. 532-33.
8. *Ibid.*, p. 535.
9. *Ibid.*, p. 537.
10. Arthur Young, *Travels*, pp. 241-42. Quoted in S.N.S. *Chung's The Theory of Share Tenancy* (Chicago, 1969), p. 34.
11. Charles Isswai, "Farm output under fixed rent and share rent tenancy", *Land Economics* (February, 1957), pp. 74-77.
12. *Ibid.*
13. Isswai supplements this view point with examples from Japan.
14. Cheung, *The Theory of Share Tenancy, op. cit.*, p. 49.
15. John W. Mellor, *The Economic of Agricultural Development* Bombay, 1969, p. 254.
16. Michael Lipton, "Towards a Theory of Land Reform", *Agrarian Reform and Agrarian Reformism*. (Ed), David Lehman (London, 1974), pp. 269-315. Similar views have also been contributed by Clive Bell "Ideology and Economic Interests in Land Reform", *Ibid.*, pp. 190-220.
17. A.K. Sen, "Peasants and Dualism with or without Surplus Labour" *Journal of Political Economy* (October, 1966), pp. 425-450.
18. S.N.S. Cheung, *The Theory of Share Tenancy, op. cit.*
19. *Ibid.*, p. 1.
20. *Ibid.*, p. 27.
21. *Ibid.*, p. 27.
22. *Ibid.*, p. 80.
23. *Ibid.*, p. 85.
24. A Chakravarty and A. Rudra -"Economic Effects of Tenancy some Negative Results". *Economic and Political Weekly* (July 14, 1973), pp. 1239-46.
25. H.N. Dwivedy and Ashok Rudra -"Economic Effects of Tenancy: Some further Results" *Economic and Political Weekly* (July 21, 1973), pp. 1291-94.
26. Bardhan P.K. and T.N. Srinivasan - "Crop sharing tenancy in Agriculture; A Theoretical Analysys," *The American Economic Review* March 1971, pp. 48-64.
27. *Ibid.*, p. 49.
28. *Ibid.*, p. 52.

29. A.K. Bagchi, "Cropsharing Tenancy and Neoclassical Economics" *Economic and Political Weekly* (January 17, 1976), pp. 74-83.
30. Krishna Bharadwaj & P.K. Das, "Tenurial Conditions and Mode of Exploitation — A Study of some villages in Orissa," *Economic and Political Weekly*, (Annual Number, February,) 1975, pp. 221-40 etc. *op. cit.*, See also A.K. Bagchi, "Crop sharing tenancy... etc." *op. cit.*
31. Krishna Bharadwaj, *Production Conditions in Indian Agriculture...* etc. *op. cit.*, pp. 1-6.
32. *Ibid.*, p. 3.
33. In such a case in order to appropriate maximum gain from the leased out area, the landlords (lessors) lease out land in smaller proportions so that the tenant would strive to maximise the productive potential of the lease parcel through employing their family labour more intensively and the increase in production would accrue to the lessor in a larger proportion. For detailed discussion see Krishna Bharadwaj, *Production Conditions in Indian Agriculture, op. cit.* pp. 51-60.
34. The gains from the production may be possible through larger utilisation of family labour or through a technical change and the landlords whether leasing out on cropsharing basis or on fixed kind/ cash rent have tried to extract more through appropriate changes in the share or fixed rents.
35. See Amit Bhaduri "A Study of Backwardness under Semifeudalism" *Economic Journal* (Vol. 83, no. 329, March, 1973).

2
HISTORICAL BACKGROUND

In the present study, we have made an attempt to analyse tenurial conditions existing in the state of Orissa. In order to place, the existing landlord-tenant relations in a historical perspective we need to study the evolution of tenurial practices in the state.

The nature of rights and obligations as between different parties having interest in land or, in short, the land tenure pattern is the result of a long evolution, determined by the socio-economic, political and geographical characteristics of a region. Therefore, it is necessary here to look into the history of the state under study, Orissa, in order to consider the factors that have influenced the growth and evolution of the land tenure practices in the state.

Orissa was under different political administration during different periods and all those had no doubt some impact on the land tenure practices and agrarian relations. But for our purpose we shall confine ourselves to a study of the evolution of tenurial conditions since the advent of the British administration.

With the grant of the Dewani of Bengal, Bihar and Orissa in 1765, Orissa was brought under the British administration. In 1765, the Dewani included but a small part of Orissa. However, by 1803, a major portion of the state was brought under the British rule.[1] The colonial administration was primarily interested in the collection of revenue and modified the hitherto existing agrarian relations in order to fulfil the objectives of obtaining maximum revenue by quick and expeditious methods.[2] Therefore, the Government decided to make settlements by auction. Estates were, therefore, auctioned and given to the highest bidder. Thus originated a class of intermediaries between the Government and the actual cultivators. These landlords had the rights of land management and were responsible to the Government for the payment of a certain fixed sum of revenue regularly. More often than not many of these landlords were speculators and had interests predominantly of commercial nature. Since, they were inexperienced in this field and had entered the agrarian economy mainly as speculators,[3] collection of revenue became very irregular and started dwindling too. Consequently, the British administrators wanted to institute an alternative system without bringing in a drastic change in the land tenure system which would affect the whole agrarian structure. But lack of landholding records was a major hindrance to resort to some alternative method of land revenue collection. Therefore, the British administration preferred to continue the collection of revenue through agents who would be approved in a different manner.

Permanent Settlement Act and Its Impact

The primary consideration to go in for an alternative system (just before the beginning of the 19th century) was to regularise the collection of revenue. Importance was also given to agricultural improvement in order to ensure necessary conditions by which the potentially vast Indian market could be conquered for British industry. The objective was to gear up the Indian agriculture to the needs of British industry and to create a market in India for their finished manufactured materials.[4] In Bengal, the system of land revenue agricultural improvement was sought to be promoted through the landed aristocracy with whom the rights of private property in the soil were vested. Permanent Settlement Act was, therefore, introduced in 1793 in these areas by which estates were settled with the *zamindars*. Here, we are not entering into a detailed critique of the effects of Permanent Settlement Act but restrict our observations to its more important effects on tenurial conditions.

When the estates were settled with the *zamindars* there emerged two different categories of areas—the permanently settled areas and temporarily settled areas.[5] By Regulation XII of the Act 1805, the whole body of revenue agents were styled as *zamindars*. These persons in charge of collection of rents in the temporarily settled estates became landholders who had the power to manage land but no power however, to increase the rent. In the permanently settled areas, another class of landlords mainly the descendants of noble families were allowed to enjoy estates. These apart, there was a class of village chiefs who enjoyed estates at a quit rent.

These landlords and *zamindars* both in the permanently settled areas and temporarily settled areas came to own vast tracts of land. Both superior landlords (those who owned estates directly from the Government) and inferior landlords (those who were a class of tenure holders and protected cultivators) were intermediaries who started subletting their land to the large mass of tenants, who either had no land of their own or were owning very small parcels of land. Consequently, a class was created, whose source of income was the rent from leased out parcels.

In a backward economy like Orissa, agriculture was the only source of living in the rural areas. Therefore, the landless and the very small farmers came to depend heavily upon leasing in lands in order to make their operational holding a viable economic holding and to raise their subsistence. The tenants in such a situation were at the mercy of the landlords and were bound by a sense of gratitude whenever they obtained a piece of land on lease. Landlords used this weak economic position of tenants as an opportunity to increase the rent. These landlords not only extracted exorbitant rents but also asked the tenants to render free or under paid labour services. The situation became worse with increasing population since it increased the demand for land. It further strengthened the position of landlords in the land market.

Thus, the expectations of the British administration that the Permanent Settlement Act would improve the landlord-tenant nexus and might induce increase in productivity, proved to have been falsified. The expectation that the Act would create a stimulus for industry, enterprise and self-reliance among the agriculturists was almost defeated.[6] The tenurial conditions contrary to expectations deteriorated further.

Later Improvement on the Permanent Settlement Act

Due to the exploitative nature of the landlord or the *zamindars*, their relationship with tenants was strained. The *zamindars* were virtually a class of feudal lords, interested only in their share of the total produce taken as rent for the plot of land leased out to tenants for cultivation for a fixed tenure. Landlords were generally interested in maximising the rent without contributing anything towards land improvement that would help in increasing agricultural productivity. Tenants in many cases failed to pay the exorbitant rent demanded by landlords. Therefore, there were large scale evictions of tenants. The Governor-General-in-Council was subsequently empowered to proclaim necessary orders to protect the tenantry and to establish a relationship between landlords and tenants in conformity with the conditions agreed upon in the 'Kabuliyat'. The underlying intention was that it would prevent rackrenting and also help the landlords in appropriating the due rent. The Act, however, had an adverse effect on tenurial relations:

> Though the Government depended on the magnanimity of the proprietors for creating a record of rights of his tenants, that is to say a record of his own obligations, they had passed the Regulation VII of 1799 giving proprietors practically unrestricted powers to distrain the crop, cattle

and other personal property of the tenant and in certain cases to arrest him for arrears of rent without reference to any court. All these drastic powers were given to him perhaps with the presumption that he would use them sparingly. For at that time, there was more land than tenants to cultivate it and nobody could believe that it would pay a proprietor to drive his tenant to despair. But the actual working of the Regulation in Bengal belied these expectations... The competition in those days were not for land but for persons to cultivate it. Consequently, if the *ryots* withheld their rents the proprietor was unable to pay the revenue... That is how estates were sold... and many new *zamindars* came and these persons — generally speculators having no traditional connection with the tenants strained these laws to the utmost for timely recovery of their rents. The Orissa *zamindars* and *ryots* did face similar calamities, but there was no help. And be it mentioned here that the idea of distraint was completely foreign and as the Rent Law Commissioner of 1880 put it, it was a mere "offset of English Law"[7]

Consequently, because of the adverse effects of the Act, the Act was withdrawn.

Act of 1859 and 1913

The rent Act of 1859 was passed defining the rights and obligations of landlords and tenants. This Act assured fair rent, restricted eviction of tenants from land in case the rent payment was regular and if the tenant was enjoying occupancy rights.[8] But in spite of this the tenants were still rackrented and evicted and the tenurial relations could not improve.

The Orissa Tenancy Act was introduced in 1913 to secure fair rent, occupancy right on land etc. This law gave protection to occupancy *ryots* to some extent but failed to give any protection to under *ryots*. One of the main obstacle in the way of the effective implementation of the Act was lack of tenurial records.

The introduction of the intermediary system of land tenure had far reaching adverse consequences on the tenurial conditions. Exorbitant rents and illegal dues, free, unpaid and under paid labour services were widely demanded by the landlords. Tenants continued to exist under the mercy of the *zamindars*. Reform measures adopted until then (1913) could not check all the abuses of irresponsible absentee landlordism which had received the sanction of the British Government. Rather it aggravated the conflict between the rich land owners and the poor landless peasantry further.[9] Such a situation continued to exist predominantly because of the underdeveloped character of the economy. Uncertainty in employment opportunities and lack of alternative source of earning compelled the tenants to stick to tenancy, irrespective of the adverse and exploitative tenurial conditions. Many of the evils of the tenurial relations that exist in the present day agrarian system owe their origin to the *zamindari* system of land tenure that existed during the colonial period.[10]

During the British rule, different parts of the present state of Orissa were having different tenurial practices. The western part of Orissa was under the control of Central Province and, therefore, the C.P. system of land tenure was prevailing in western Orissa. There were various classes of intermediaries and according to their respective interest in land they were classified as *Zamindars, Malguzars, Malik Markbuzars, Gountias* etc. Rent charged by all these intermediaries were high, generally more than fifty per cent of the gross produce. This apart free or underpaid labour services were usually asked for by the landlords.

The coastal region of the state had the *zamindari* (Bengal) system of land tenure where the *zamindars* were the agents of government and enjoyed the authority to collect the rent from the tenants to whom they leased out the land. They were all powerful, appropriating exorbitant produce rents besides free labour services rendered by the tenants.

The southern parts of the state was under the Madras Presidency. Under this system both the *zamindary* and the *Ryotwari* systems coexisted. Usually, more than fifty per cent of the gross produce was paid as rent to the lessors. Rendering unpaid labour services to the lessor was almost an essential condition with each lease.

There were twenty- four princely states in the province of Orissa, each having its own land tenure system. Besides the ruler there were a number of intermediaries — the members of the ruling family, their agents, the *Brahmattors* etc. Since, the land laws were not codified there was no guarantee of any security of the tenants. They were subjected to pay not only exorbitant rents, but also all kind of cesses[11] and unpaid labour services whenever demanded by the landlords.

Though different tenurial systems were pratised in different areas, there were some features which were found common to all the different systems and these were:

(i) The landlords were mostly exploitative by nature, charging exorbitant rents without bearing any production responsibility.

(ii) In addition to the rent appropriated, landlords were demanding free labour services and other "gifts" on different occasions.

(iii) Eviction of a tenant was a general consequence when he failed to satisfy any of these above conditions. Eviction of tenants was rampant in all these areas, particularly in the coastal districts of the state where it was conspicuous.

So far as the tenants were concerned they were, more often than not, left with but a small portion of the gross produce which was seldom sufficient even for their mere subsistence. Very often tenants were left at the mercy of the feudal landlords.

If any nation's history, then the history of the English in India is a string of futile and really absurd (in practice infamous) economic experiments. In Bengal, they crated a caricature of large scale English landed estates; in South-Eastern India a caricature of small parcelled property; in the North-East, they did all they could to transform the Indian economic community with the common ownership of the soil into a caricature of itself.[12]

So far we have discussed agrarian relations in the state prior to 1936, when Orissa was not a separate state. We find different tenurial systems prevailing in different areas, because they were under the different administrative units belonging to Bengal, Bihar, Central Province and Madras.[13] Therefore, the state of Orissa presents a peculiar conglomeration of different tenurial practices. The tenurial system was further complicated because of the existence of 24 ex-states which had no uniform but varied system of tenancy.

Orissa became a separate province in 1936. From 1937, till independence popular governments tried to redress the sufferings of the tenantry but could hardly succeed in improving the landlord-tenant relations. The evils of the tenurial systems were so deep rooted that to bring about a radical change needed a similar change in the social system. But the popular government did not envisage any radical changes.

Independence and After

Tenurial conditions remained complex even after independence. It was difficult to carry out uniform reform measures for the whole state due to diversity in land tenure practices hitherto followed in the various parts of the state. Immediately after independence the ex-state areas merged with the state, making land tenure problem even more complex.

There was another major factor which was also responsible for further complicating the situation existing in respect of leases. Even prior to 1947, it was decided as a matter of policy to abolish all intermediary interests. This actually resulted in making the landlord-tenant relation more strained. Most of the intermediaries being apprehensive of losing land and rent thereof as a consequence of land reform measures, evicted a large number of tenants. This, indeed, happened prior to the actual implementation of the Orissa Estate Abolition Act, 1951. Evictions were more rampant in coastal districts of the state where the *zamindari* system of land tenure was in practice. So, there was an immediate necessity to restrict such evictions.

Rackrenting was still persisting. Increasing population pressure combined with absence of alternative source of earning in villages left the tenants with no alternative but to accept the onerous lease terms laid down by landlords. Fear of land reform legislations and abolition of the intermediaries made the landlords more apprehensive of losing landed property. Therefore, they became cautious and choosy while selecting tenants. Tenants not known to landlords found it difficult to obtain leases. Insecurity of tenants increased as the landlords hesitated to lease out land to the same tenant for long durations. Most of the tenants were evicted from land. This increased the insecurity of the tenants and they were left at the mercy of the landlords. Thus, in the post-independence period, the tenurial conditions worsened, became more complicated and the landlord-tenant nexus became more strained.

In the post-independence period, therefore, the main objectives of land reform measures were :

(i) providing security to the tenant;
(ii) regulation of rent;
(iii) conferment of ownership rights to tenants; and
(iv) ensuring socio-economic justice through redistribution of land.

Impact of Major Land Reform Legislation During Post-Independence Period

Here, we do not intend to have a detailed discussion of the various land reform legislations adopted during the post-independence period. We will, however, give a brief but critical comments on some of the important land reform legislation enacted in the post-independence period and their impact on the landlord-tenant nexus and on the lease market as a whole. We have mentioned earlier about the strained relationship between the landlord and the tenant and the large scale evictions following thereupon. This happened, primarily because landlords were apprehensive of losing land or rent thereof because of the land reform legislations enacted immediately after independence.

The Orissa Tenants Protection Act was passed as a first step in 1948 in order to restrict large scale eviction. The Act had provisions for restricting eviction of tenants by landlords possessing more than 33 acres of land and for regulating the payment of rent by setting a prescribed limit. The rent payable by any tenant having occupancy rights was prescribed to be within the limit of one third of the gross produce; in case of Ganjam and Koraput districts, a tenant holding land on produce rent was to pay only one-sixth of the gross produce as rent; tenant without any security of tenure were not bound to pay more than two-fifth of the gross produce as rent. Primarily, the Act was introduced in the coastal districts but subsequently, it was substituted by a more comprehensive legislation — The Orissa Tenants' Protection and Relief Act, 1955 — covering all tenants of the state. But both the acts did not have any appreciable effects in improving the tenurial conditions. This was mainly because of certain loopholes in the Acts — first, the clause that landlords with less than 33 acres could evict tenants proved to be an advantage to landlords in carrying out evictions. Holdings of 33 acres or more were rare when the Act was enforced. In the coastal districts of the state particularly, most of the land holdings were below this limit.[14] Therefore, eviction of tenants was easy within the legal limits. Moreover, under the provisions of the Act landlord had the right to resume land for personal cultivation,[15] to an aggregate extent of 7 standard acres.[16] This provision was widely misused. Land ostensibly resumed for personal cultivation again was leased out on a share-cropping or fixed rent system, where tenants were treated either as labourers or as partners in cultivation though the landlord never shared cost of production.[17] By definition, cultivation of land by servants or hired labourers is included under "personal" cultivation. In many cases, landlords managed to get a bond signed by actual tenants to prove that these tenant cultivators were not tenants but labourers hired to cultivate the land under the supervision of landlords from whom they had leased in the land parcel.

To confer ownership right to the actual tiller, as a first step, the Estate Abolition Act was passed in 1952. It was assumed that conferment of such right would bring about a significant change in the level and volume of production,[18] and that this would result in a major redistribution of rural income "to the advantage of those who work in the field and to the disadvantage of those who do not".[19] Abolition of intermediary rights was no doubt a complex problem. In the coastal region of the state, the intermediary interest between the state and the actual tiller of the soil sometimes number quite as many as six or seven.[20] After the enactment of the Estate Abolition Act in the ex-state areas, intermediaries as a class or non-cultivating owners based on share-cropping started dwindling.[21] Traditional *zamindars* lost their previously enjoyed prestige, position and along with it the social status. However, the rentiers still persisted as a class subsisting on the surplus appropriated through exorbitant produce rents and enjoying the unpaid free labour services from the actual tillers of the soil. A more comprehensive Act was passed in 1960 which provided for rationalisation of land tenure patterns by abolishing intermediary interest and for ensuring social justice and equity by way of fixing ceilings on land holdings. But in spite of this Act, large scale subletting of land still continued in different guises and a class of new landlordism with different ways of concealed tenancy came into existence. Holders of title in land who were tenants to the Government in turn sublet their land and became landlords over the subtenants.[22] Being pressurised by landlords and apprehensive of eviction, tenants did not try to establish their rights of possession over the leased in land. The enactment of Reform Laws in the post-independence period resulted in making the agrarian relations more complex. Landlord-tenant nexus had become more strained and intricate. In order to evade, the impact of land legislation, landlords resorted to various methods for leasing out land because of which the real extent of tenancy is concealed. Landlords had tried using all their resources and their socio-economic position to maintain the status quo.

In the landlease market, there is a large mass of tenants eager to lease in land. Their position becomes worse because of the inelastic supply of land and secondly because of the backward nature of our village economy, where employment opportunities other than agriculture are very very limited. Therefore, they are left with no alternative but to accept the terms of lease laid down by the landlords while leasing in land parcels. The old pattern of feudal landlordism appears to be still persisting in most of the villages of Orissa. The tenants do not have sufficient strength to fight against exploitative situations created because of the peculiar features of the land market (which we will discuss in the following chapters). Thus, the situation has not improved much in the post-independence period despite various land reform legislations enacted in recent years.

The landlord-tenant relationship discussed here is only a broad and general presentation of predominant facts and lacks detailed information which we think is crucial for an analytical study of the tenurial questions — to understand the functioning of the lease market and to know how the landlord-tenant relationship has been governed by their respective resource position and the socio-economic status of both landlords and tenants. The questions like who leases from whom, on what terms and conditions, and what variations occur in lease terms depending on the changing agro-economic and technical conditions are highly significant and are of prime importance to analyse the complex character of the lease market and therefore, need to be investigated.

Hence, in the next few chapters, we will discuss the crucial factors influencing the lease market such as who leases in from whom and the existing lease patterns in the different areas, i.e. irrigated, unirrigated, cash crop and tribal areas, the motivational factors that determine the lease; the preference in selection of tenants and the variations in the terms and conditions that have occurred recently. We shall discuss all these factors using the data and other information collected through a personal survey of eleven villages spread over different parts of the state of Orissa at two different points of time — first one in 1974-75 and the second one covering again the same households in the early 90s.

REFERENCES

1. Some parts of Balasore district of Orissa state were under the British administration by 1760. The remaining parts of the districts of Cuttack, Puri and Balasore (except Banki Sub-Division which came under the British rule in 1840) came under the British control in 1803.
2. S.C. Gupta, *Agrarian Relations and Early British Rule in India* (Bombay, 1963), p. 2.
3. *Land Tenure and Land Reforms in Orissa*. (Board of Revenue, Government of Orissa, 1962), p. 3 and p. 7.
4. S.C. Gupta, *op. cit.*, p. 2.
5. Permanently settled status were given to the *zamindars* of the ancient *killas* which lay on the coast or bordering the tributary *Mahals*. Khurda was later resumed as result of the revolt by

the *Raja* and became a Government estate, out of which the *Ekhrajat Mahal*, a revenue free state was granted to provide for the upkeep of Shri Jagnnath Temple of Puri. The rest of the areas covered by the districts of Balasore, Cuttack and Puri were not brought under permanent settlement, but were subject to annual and triennial settlement.

6. See Romesh Dutt, *The Economic History of India*, Vol. II (Delhi, 1970), p. 217.
7. *Land Tenure and Land Reforms in Orissa, op. cit.*, p. 7.
8. The Bengal Tenancy Act 1885, provided that every tenant who had held land for twelve continuous years acquires thereby a right of occupancy. The non-occupancy tenants cannot be ejected except by execution of a degree of a competent court nor can their rent be enhanced at shorter intervals than five years.
9. R.K. Mukherjee, *Land Problem in India*, (Calcutta 1933) See also *Replies to the Questionnaires issued by the Land Revenue Commission, Bengal* (Calcutta 1939), pp. 98-99; also *Report of the Congress Agrarian Reforms Committee* (New Delhi, 1951).
10. "The mistake of the Permanent Settlement was that the *zamindars* who were only landholders, were identified with the English landlords, real proprietors, and the rights of the tenants were" in the words of Field, "so completely affected that at present it is difficult to find a single vestige or ascertain what they were. This mistake subsequently was repeated in more than one province. The Government first created middle man, called them landlords and wresting some of these to the landlords as guarantee to punctual payment of *Kist* of the *Sarkar*. The Government by forced sale and attachment reduced most of the great *zamindars* of Bengal during the period of about 20 years following the settlement to distress and beggery, the Government then gave the power of distraint copied from English law, to the *zamindars* to relieve their 'distress' which powers they scandalously abused." R.K. Mukherjee, *op.cit.*, pp. 49-50; see also Romesh Dutt, *op. cit.*, vol. I, pp. 37-38, and *The Replies to the British Indian Association to the Questionnaires issued by the Land Revenue Commission Bengal, op. cit.*, pp.17-40.
11. "For instance, in some parts of Orissa, Sir W.W. Hunter found that the tenants had to pay, besides their customary rents, 33

different cesses, they paid whenever their children married, they paid for fee to erect embankments, to grow sugarcane, to attend festival of Jagannath etc. (Orissa I, 55-59)" - Alfred Marshall, *Principles of Economics* (London, 1972), p. 533 (footnote).

12. Karl Marx, *Capital,* Vol. II (Moscow, 1971), pp. 333-34. See also Marshall, *op.cit.*, p. 534; Romesh Dutt, *op.cit.,* pp. 37-40; R. K. Ramdhyani, *op.cit.,* Vol. I, pp. 55-57 and S.C. Gupta, *op. cit.*
13. Prior to 1st April 1936, the date on which the province of Orissa was created, the districts of Cuttack, Puri, Balasore, Sambalpur and Angul as they existed on 1st March 1936, formed the Orissa Division of the Province of Bihar and Orissa. Sambalpur was originally a part of Bengal till 1862 when it was transferred to the Central Provinces. In 1905, it was transferred to Orissa Division of the then Bengal Presidency. The present districts of Ganjam and Koraput and the Balliguda Sub-Division of Boudh Phulbani which has been a part of Madras Presidency were transferred to Orissa on 1st April 1936. Similarly the Khariai *ex-zamindary* and the Mahadevapalli police station were transferred to Orissa from the Central Provinces and Berar on 1st April 1936. *Land Tenure and Land Reforms in Orissa, op.cit.*, p. 1.
14. S. Misra, *Economic Survey of Orissa*, Vol. I (Cuttack 1961), p.149. See also B. Misra, and B. Jena "Working of the two tenancy laws in Orissa", *Indian Journal of Agricultural Economics* (April-June 1957), pp.117-120.
15. Personal Cultivation means cultivation by one's own labour or with the assistance of labour or with the assistance of a member of that family *or a servant or hired labour on payment of wages in cash or in kind* but not by way of share in the produce of the land under one's personal supervision or that of any member of the family.
16. A standard acre means one acre of wet land or two acres of dry land.
17. B.R. Karla, "Land Reform Legislation and its implementation in different states, " *Indian Journal of Agricultural Economics*, (January-March 1962, Conference Number), pp.144-153.
18. There are many writings arguing that owner-cultivated farms are more productive than tenant cultivated farms. We have already discussed some of these views in Chapter 1.
19. Daniel Thorner, *Agrarian Prospects of India* (University

Press, Delhi, 1956), p. 79.

20. *Report of the Administrative Enquiry Committee* (Government of Orissa, 1958), Vol. I, p. 57.
21. There were altogether three lakhs of estates which were to be vested in the Government. The progress was not remarkable in the initial stage. Later reports show that except 2,312 all estates have been vested in the Government. *Ibid.*, p. 69. See also, *Replies to the Questionnaire on Land Reforms, issued by the National Commission on Agriculture*, Government of Orissa, 1972.
22. V.K.R.V. Rao, "Valedictory address" in the *Seminar on Land Reforms*, (Socio-Economic Research Division, Planning Commission. New Delhi, 1966), pp. 31-36.

3
LEASE PATTERNS

In the preceding chapter, we have discussed some of the major historical factors that influenced the evolution of the landlord-tenant nexus. We take up here a more detailed analysis of the prevailing land lease patterns to bring out the nature and the structure of the lease market. Studies on tenancy particularly in relation to nature and structure of the lease market in Orissa are lacking and the available literature are not adequate in giving information which we assume are crucial for an intensive analysis of tenurial relations. Therefore, it is essential to analyse the peculiar features of the lease market that influence the tenurial relations.

Some Salient Features of the Lease Market

The lease market in the state appears to be largely non-integrated because of the skewed distribution of landholdings by ownership. This iniquitous distribution of landholding is the result of certain historical and socio-economic factors and is consequently responsible for the existence and continuance of some of the tenancy practices already referred to. In a backward economy like Orissa agriculture is the major source of livelihood and land is the major form wealth. In the rural areas, therefore, the desire to hold land is extremely acute. The whole pattern of social power and prestige as well as one's overall economic well being depends upon the access to land. But the extent of land that is available for cultivation and its distribution among various categories of households having interest in land are important considerations that determine the patterns of the lease market. The imperfection in the lease market whatever exists today owes its origin to this inequitous distribution of land in the lease market. With unequal distribution of various types households by ownership such as households who do not own any land i.e. the landless, the marginal landholders who own vary negligible parcels of land, the small, semi - medium, medium size landholders and households owning large size landholdings. We notice that more than two - thirds of the households who are marginal farmers own about 20 per cent of land while 0.6 per cent of landowners own about 6 per cent of land. If we include, both large and medium size class land owners (we have another category of semi-medium size class) we find that less than 8 per cent of such landowners own nearly 26 per cent of land. This clearly explains the iniquity that exists in the land market. About 8 per cent of the total households are landless. These are estimates made by the National Sample Survey. But in reality, the number of landless households may be still higher. It is worth noting here the percentage distribution of households having interest in land. We note that more that two third of the total households are either landless or marginal landholders while the large and medium size landholders are even less than 4 per cent of the total number of households. Most of these large and medium size landholders do not undertake personal cultivation of land because of several reasons. Households belonging to upper castes do not undertake personal cultivation, service holders or people engaged in secondary or tertiary occupations do not cultivate. These are abscentee landlords who lease out land. Similary very poor households do not have any resources to undertake personal cultivation and therefore, they have to lease out their land parcels under distress, we notice the preponderance of a large mass of landless, marginal and small landholders who are eager to lease in land parcels to satisfy their minimum subsistence needs. While only a few possess land that can be leased out to be cultivated by tenant farmers, there remains a large mass of households who are eager to lease in. This indeed is responsible not only for the imperfection of the land market but also for the existence of exploitative tenurial conditions in the lease market. The landlords successfully manipulate lease terms in their favour taking advantage of the weak economic position of the land hungry tenants. The intricacies of the lease market can be revealed further when we make a more detailed analysis of the supply and demand sides of the lease market.

Categories of Households	*Percentage of Households*
Landless	7.67
Marginal	58.39
Small	20.84
Semi-medium	9.31
medium	3.42
Large	0.37

Supply Side of the Land Market and the Types of Lessors

On the supply side of the land lease market, we find that a major proportion of the lease area is supplied by large landowners. One of reasons may be that these landowners find it difficult to bring all the scattered and tiny fragmented plots under personal cultivation. (Fragmentation owes its origin to a number of institutional and socio-economic factors like the existence of Hindu joint family which when gets divided, the landholding also gets divided and thus with each division, the land unit becomes smaller. Similarly, when small peasants borrow in order to meet their consumption needs, sometimes either they mortgage a part of their owned landholdings or sell it to the creditor to avail of a loan). There is also a class of landlords, who engage themselves in the non-agricultural sector and therefore, have to lease out. There are also landlords who lease out because of their physical disability. Above all, there are traditional landlords who lease out since they do not undertake personal cultivation either because of caste barriers or because of family prestige and their status in the society. These may be either big landholders or small or marginal landholders.

This process of leasing out by large landowners and leasing in by small landholders may be supposed to bring about a more egaliterian distribution in terms of operational holdings. In fact, this would be presumed under a so called perfectly competitive lease market. But the lease market here does not appear to be a competitive one in order to ensure such an egalitarian distribution of operational holding.

We observe that lessors who constitute the supply side of the lease market are not always large landowners. Among them there are very small landowners, too. It is very significant to note that landlords with less than one acre or between one to two acres of land in their possession are found to be in significant number as lessors. Of the total households leasing out land about 56 per cent are marginal land owners followed by 28 percent of households who are small landholders.[2] Such a trend is to be viewed seriously because this goes against the objective of egalitarian distribution of landholding. There may be various reasons for which these small landholders lease out their entire holding. There are also some households who are lessors, because they are employed in the non-farming sector. But in this case too, the lessors cannot always be classified as belonging to well-to-do sections of the society. The fact that they rent out their land has no bearing whatsoever on any desire to live as rent receivers. Lessees in these case are in all probability, economically better of than the non-agricultural labouring class.

Demand Side of the Lease Market and the Different Types of Lessees

On the demand side of the lease market, we also find not

only small farmers but medium and large cultivators and landowners too, who desire to lease in land. The motive for leasing in is primarily to increase the operational holding and making cultivation more economically viable and profitable. Thus, we find there are well-to-do farmers who quite often are keen to lease in. Landowners occupying 10 acres or above land of their own may be considered as fairly well-to-do farmers in the state and these are the households who are seen to be leasing in land in order to increase their operational holdings to make agriculture a profitable concern.

Conclusions alike have also been drawn in Dash's study.[3] The semi-medium landowners appear to be more effective in leasing in land. Of the total area leased out this category of better off households lease in a considerable amount of land. Therefore, the general notion that lessees are only the small and marginal landholders does not appear to be true. The medium category of farmers have also penetrated into the lease market and prove to be more effective as lessees.

An egalitarian distribution of land in terms of operational holding would have been possible under the assumption of a perfectly competitive lease market. But we see the lease market seems to be biased infavour of a particular group of lessees. On the supply side, it is seen that while leasing out, lessors consider several factors like the initial resource position of the tenant. The resource position is usually reflected in the amount of land that one owns, and one's access to market, like credit and other factor inputs. It is expected that these lessees possess more resources which they can invest in land and therefore, can pay more rent regulary. But more or less it is the tenant who owns some amount of land and also leases in some amount of land to increase his operational holding is generally considered to be better off than one who does not own any land. Therefore, we find that it is the cultivating owners who are able to lease in more land. This argument is supplemented further when we notice the distribution of leased in area among the tenants in various size categories by taking the data provided by the Farm Management Studies for the districts of Cuttack and Sambalpur.[4] The agricultural census of the state of Orissa,[5] also corroborates this broad conclusion. Those who own some amount of land are seen to be comparatively more effective as lessees than those who do not own any land or own larger parcels of land.

Thus, it is noticed that there exists a bias in favour of the households who own some amount of land, have better access to the factor market like credit etc. They are more effective are lessees. The effective is leasing in of land has two important elements: one, the *desirability* of leasing in and second, the *feasibility* of leasing in land. While the non-owing cultivators may desire to lease in they have less capacity to do so since. Their access to the factor market is limited and owned non-land resources being very insignificant their ability to invest in land is restricted. At the same time, we find also the landowners with considerable amount of owned land may not be preferred as lessees because lessors, while leasing out presume that the big owner-tenants (tenant cultivators who own considerable amount of land) may neglect relatively the leased in land and prefer to deploy resources on their own land[6] so that they entirely reap the benefits of inputs invested in their own land.

Thus, the tenants already operating some land i.e. the owner-tenants with small owned holding and pure tenants who have already leased in some land seem to be preferred to other categories of tenants. This is because these two categories of tenants are expected to take sincere interest in increasing the productivity of land because their share of the produce will be more after the rentals are paid to the landowner. Even though the other categories of tenants are interested to lease in land, their mere desire to lease in land is not enough in order to be effective to lease in more land. Tenants should be able to pay more rent to the lessors. It is these tenants who are capable to paying more by putting in best of the resources available with them.

Imperfections in the Lease Market

The above discussions show how the commonly assumed fact that lessors are generally prosperous landowners and tenants are poor cultivators is not always true. On the otherhand, we also find that the land lease market does not bring about an egalitarian distribution of operational holding. In the lease market, some of the lessors appear to be dominating the supply side and some of the lessees seem to be the most effective as lessors in. In the former case, the big land-owners who supply a large portion of the leased out area in the lease market predominate the supply side while on the demand side, tenants who are economically somewhat better off than the landless or have some land to operate upon seem to be most effective as lessees. The economically better off tenants enjoy a favourable bargaining strength in the lease market than the very small tenants. Thus, the lease market appears to be an imperfect one where we find characteristics of monopolistic and monopsonistic market conditions coexist.

Therefore, in order to study the peculiar structure of the lease market and the behaviour of lessors and lessees taking part in the lease transactions it becomes essential here to enquire into the questions like 'who leases from whom' and factors influencing each lease contract. The landlord-tenant relation under any land tenure system can be better understood if it is analysed in terms of their relative resource position. Studies analysing tenurial relations have either failed to take account of the particular ways the agrarian markets function or have been based on informations reflecting only partially the question of tenancy. The actual functioning of any lease market cannot be studied in isolation. In an economy, where employment opportunities are highly uncertain, the distribution of landed property is highly iniquitous, the initial resource position of the landlord and tenant and their links with markets like credit, employment etc. seem to largely influence the landlord-tenant nexus. We have seen on the demand side the existence of tenants who in the absence of any better alternative are compelled to lease in tiny parcels of land for their mere survival at onerous lease conditions. Access to credit market being limited, tenants might be forced to borrow from their respective landlords who in turn try to exploit the tenants either through extracting exorbitant rents or unpaid or underpaid labour services, or by stipulating crop production. This is largely due to their weak economic position that these tenants are subjected to such exploitative situations. On the supply side of the lease market, we note that landlords, particularly the large land owners because of their batter economic status (compared to the tenants to whom they lease out land) enjoy the option to whom to lease out and in what parcels and very often lay down terms and conditions of the lease to the disadvantage of the lessees. Therefore, it is the relative resource position (both labour and non-labour) of tenants and landlords combined with other socio-economic status and the various motivational factors determining the leasing in and leasing out of land significantly influence the landlord-tenant relation. Hence, it is essential to study the tenurial relation in terms of the relative resource strength of different landlords and tenants. The available literature, however, does not give sufficient information in this regard,[7] and as such does not reveal the true features of the functioning of the land lease market and lease pattern, lease terms and conditions and factors which largely mould the agrarian relations.

In the present study, an attempt has been made to analyse some of the crucial factors influencing the lease market.[8] In order to know the lease pattern, lease terms and conditions and factors that influence each lease unit, we have studied each tenant in relation to his landlord or landlords from whom he has leased in the land parcels. We have surveyed eleven villages in the state of Orissa and in all such villages, we have covered all those households who are either leasing in or leasing out land. This helps not only to obtain a complete picture of the lease patterns that exist in the different villages but also to note the peculiarities of lease terms that exist within a village. We could also note the differences in lease terms between one tenant and landlord pair with another. Such a matrix of landlord-tenant also makes it easy to analyse factors that might have been responsible for the prevalence of peculiarities in the lease market.

We have collected information from the same landlords and tenant households at two different points of time — first one in the year 1974-75 the second in early 90s (after a period of one and half decades) in order to see how changes in the infrastructure, availability of better inputs and adoption of better techniques of production have brought about a transition in the lease terms and conditions, lease patterns and changes in the mode of exploitation.

Selection of Sample Villages

All the eleven villages have been selected purposively from different parts of Orissa State. As it has already been pointed out, the problem of tenancy is peculiar and complex since various parts of the present state of Orissa were under different administrative regimes.[9] Therefore, we have purposively selected the villages in order to bring out the differences in the tenurial practices followed in different parts. Moreover, Orissa can be divided into two distinct regions: one, the 'coastal region' consisting of the districts of Balasore, Cuttack, Puri and Ganjam;[10] and the other 'inland region' comprising the rest of the districts of the state. The coastal region of the state has irrigation facilities since long and is more fertile. The area lies in the deltaic range. The inland region was less developed until independence. Most of these areas were jungles, were not easily accessible and therefore, were thinly populated.

Irrigation facilities were absent in most parts of these districts and cultivation largely depended upon the monsoon. Some of these districts were inhabited mostly by tribals, where shifting cultivation was in practice (even now they follow the same method of cultivation in some parts). Only in the 60s after the construction of the Hirakund Dam and the canals some parts of the region have irrigation facilities and have started cultivating High Yielding Variety (HYV) of paddy, utilising fertiliser, pesticides etc. Thus, the two regions have distinctive characteristics therefore, in order to study the changing patterns of tenurial relations and to bring out the regional differences we have purposively selected some villages from both the coastal and the inland regions.

Further in order to focus on certain peculiarities of agro-economic conditions, we have included in our selection some villages which are irrigated, some unirrigated, villages producing cash crops, and some belonging to the tribal areas from different parts of the State.

Brief Introduction to the Sample Villages

The villages having irrigation facilities have been selected from the coastal as well as from the inland region. The sample village Lunahar is from the coastal deltaic region, and has canal irrigation facilities since long. The village was under the Bengal Presidency and was previously under the *zamindary* system of land tenure. The other villages Attabira, Parmanpur and Babebira are from the *western* parts of Orissa. Irrigation facilities were extended to these villages in the late sixties after the construction of Hirakund Dam on the river Mohanadi at Samabalpur. These villages were under the Central Province and were under the Gountia system of land tenure.

We have selected villages having no irrigation facilities in a similar manner. The village Balarampur of Cuttack district is from the coastal region, was in the Bengal Presidency under the *zamindary* system of land tenure. The other village Bhalliamunda is from the inland region and is in Bolangir district, earlier belonging to ex-state area.

We have surveyed another village, Nalabanta which is from the district of Ganjam, lying in the coastal region. This village produces cash crop namely sugarcane.

We have in our sample four villages from two districts which have considerable proportion of tribal population. From Mayurbhanja district, two villages have been selected while the other predominantly tribal villages are Gumagarh, G. Udayagiri and Raikia from Phulbani district.

Selection of Households

In all these villages, we have covered almost all households, who either lease out or lease in land or do both i.e. they lease out and simultaneously lease in. These households were divided into four distinct groups:

(i) Pure landlords : these are the households who only lease out;

(ii) Tenant landlords : those who lease out some land and simultaneously lease in, but are *net* lessors;

(iii) Pure tenants : these are the households who do not possess any land of their own and their operational holdings consist of leased in land only;

(iv) Owner tenants : those who possess some land and also lease in, but are *net* lessees.

Size-Wise Classification of the Households

In order to take account of the possible size effect, we have divided the households in each category into three size groups — small upto 3 acres, medium 3-8 acres, and big above 8 acres.

The size classes are of rather uneven intervals as there are only a few large holdings. We have tried to rectify the bias arising because of arbitrary divisions (especially, in the size group of more than 8 acres) by providing later a more detailed breakdown according to more size groups. We have already given in Table 3.1 frequency distribution of households — landlords (i.e. lessors) and tenants (i.e. lessees) by the above three categories. Here by size of holding we mean operational holding in the cases of all categories except the landlords, where it refers to ownership holding. In our discussion, we have dropped the category (ii) since there is only one tenant-landlord in our sample.

The Landlords

In these eleven villages, we surveyed 80 landlords in all; of these, 24 are small landlords of whom we find 10 in the tribal villages. In the unirrigated areas this category of small landlords, though not very significant cannot be ignored, since they are more in number than the big landlords. Majority of the landlords lease out all their land and very few of them, 11 out of 80, hold a part of the holding for self-cultivation. We will discuss later the various motivational factors influencing landlords in leasing out land. But we can briefly state here that these small landlords leasing out land mostly under distress conditions, incapable of undertaking self-cultivation because of their limited economic resources. In all these areas including the villages having irrigation facilities we find many of the small landowners leasing out their entire owned holding to tenants and themselves working as wage labourers. Out of 80 lessors, there are 35 who are medium class landowners. Landlords of this class appear significantly in the cash crop areas. In the unirrigated regions, too, we find similar class of lessors in the medium size holdings. These are mostly absentee landowners.

There are 21 landlords owning more than 8 acres of land, mostly in the irrigated region and in the cash crop areas. They

TABLE : 3.1

Frequency Distribution of Households by Categories

	Irrigated Area (No.)	*Unirrigated Area (No.)*	*Cash Crop Area (No.)*	*Tribal Area (No.)*	*Total (No.)*
Pure Tenants					
Small	10	3	7	6	26
Medium	4	-	1	1	6
Big	4	-	-	-	4
Owner-Tenants					
Small	9	3	7	13	32
Medium	6	17	10	12	45
Big	-	3	-	3	6
Landlords					
Small	8	6	-	10	24
Medium	3	11	17	4	35
Big	6	5	8	2	21
Total	50	48	50	51	199

Small : upto 3 acres; Medium: 3 to 8 acres; Big : above 8 acres.

lease out land under varying circumstances. While the landlords in the cash crop areas lease out largely because they are 'traditional' landlords, in the irrigated areas they lease out because it is more lucrative. We will deal with these motivational factors in more detail in the following chapter.

In our sample, we have eleven landlords who lease out a part of the owned land and keep some for self-cultivation, the rest 69 landowners leasing out the entire amount of land they own.

The Tenants

Among the tenants, we have both pure and owner-tenants. Both categories of tenants have been divided into three different size classes — small with an operational holding of below 3 acres, medium and big operating land between 3-8 acres and 8 acres or more respectively. In the category of pure tenants, we have more tenants in the small size group. In all, there are 36 pure tenants, out of which 26 belong to the small size group. Small pure tenants are significant in all types of sample villages but more particularly so in the irrigated region. In all, there are 83 owner-tenants. We find them to be more significant in the small and medium sizes 77 in number (See Table 3.1)

Looking at the distribution of tenants in the different size classes, we find two striking features. Among the pure tenants the small tenants with small operational holdings appear to be more prominent while among owner tenants, the medium class tenants predominate. Predominance of tenants in the small size class may be due to particular preference of landlords to lease out land in small parcels to a large number of small tenants. Some of the landlords appear to presume that such a process of leasing out would increase their social status in terms of number of tenants under them and may also enable them to gain more of free labour services which generally accompany conditions of lease.[11]

The reason for the predominance of medium and

smallowner tenants in the land lease market may be because of the fact that these tenant cultivators, as expected by the landlords, (on the basis of experience), would cultivate the leased in land more intensively. Although, the non-labour resources of the small tenant families are limited, they use their family labour power more intensively in the cultivation of the leased in land. In case of an owner-tenant, generally speaking, the tenant may be interested in cultivating the owned land more intensively (particularly when the owned land is substantially large) whereas in the case of a pure tenant, the tenant will put in the family labour entirely to the cultivation of the leased in land. This will be so because in the former case the owner-tenant will appropriate whatever he produces on his own land, whereas the produce on the leased in land will be shared by the lessor and lessee. The total return to labour and capital applied to the leased and land will not accrue entirely to the tenant farmer. Further, it may be argued that his interest to invest in the leased in plot will be restricted. Though, the produce is similarly shared in case of a pure tenant, the tenant farmer in this case tries to intensively cultivate the land because alternative source of livelihood in his case is almost absent. Whatever he gets from the leased in land after the landlord is paid his share, remains as the sole source of living for his entire family. Alternative source to eke out of a living being completely absent he has no alternative but to put in his entire family labour power to maximise the output and in the process the landlord enjoys the benefit. Similar would be the case of an owner-tenant cultivator whose owned holding is too small and his livelihood depends crucially on the lease. Hence, we notice lessors leasing out mostly to tenants operating in the small and medium size holdings, whether pure or owner-tenant.

All these indicate the complex nature of the lease market. Therefore, in order to analyse the peculiarities of the land lease market it becomes necessary to study tenants in relation to their landlords in order to know how the initial resource position of the lesses and the lessors influence the lease terms, and the lease pattern.

Who Leases from Whom

Table 3.2 gives us the lessor-lessee matrix which shows who leases from whom. In the sample, we have divided the tenants and the landlords into different size class in order to know who are the tenants leasing in from lessors of what size class and who are the lessors leasing out to which class of tenants and of what category. In our sample, there are landlords who have leased out to more than one tenant. Similarly, it also includes tenants who have leased in from more than one landlord. Therefore, the lease units are numerically more than the actual numbers of landlords and tenants surveyed. The Table 3.2 shows that among the lessees the medium size owner-tenants predominate, followed by pure and owner - tenants in the small size group. It can be seen that there are a sizeable number of small landowners who are leasing out. While the small and medium size landowners lease out predominantly to tenants operating in the medium size holdings the big landowners lease out generally to tenants with small operational holdings.

We have given a more detailed break up of landlords and tenants in more size groups in order to bring out the size distribution more clearly. We have recorded the ownership holding of landlords (lessors) along the columns and the operational holdings of the tenants (pure tenants as well as owner-tenants) along the rows. The entries in parenthesis denote the number of pure tenants and those without are the number of owner-tenants in the respective lessor-lessee groups.

In Table 3.2, we give the frequency distribution of lease units according to the lessee-lessor groups of all villages. We note a cluster of tenants in the size class of below 8 acres holdings. A

TABLE : 3.2

Frequency Distribution of Lease Units According to Lessee-Lessor Group—All Village

	Small Landlords (Upto 3 acres)	*Medium Landlords (3.8 acres)*	*Big Landlords (8 + acres)*	*Total*
Pure Tenants				
Small	8	11	19	38
Medium	7	4	10	21
Big	3	4	6	13
Owner-Tenants				
Small	7	15	19	41
Medium	27	44	24	95
Big	5	1	8	14
Total	57	79	86	222

Small : Upto 3 acres; Medium : 3 to 8 acres; Big : above 8 acres.

TABLE : 3.3

Frequency of Lease Units According to Lessee—Lessor—All Villages

Operational Holding of Tenants (Acres) \ *Ownership Holding of Landlords (Acres)*	*0-3*	*3-6*	*6-8*	*8-12*	*12-20*	*20+*	*Total*
0-3	7	8	7	4	10	5	41
	(8)	(4)	(7)	(6)	(10)	(3)	(38)
3-6	17	21	11	6	7	5	67
	(5)	(1)	(2)	(1)	(4)	(3)	(16)
6-8	10	7	5	2	1	3	28
	(2)	-	(1)	-	(1)	(1)	(5)
8-12	2	1	-	-	2	3	8
12+	3	-	-	1	2	-	6
	(3)	(1)	(3)	(1)	(2)	(3)	(13)
Total	39	37	23	13	22	16	150
	(18)	(6)	(13)	(8)	(17)	(10)	(72)

Note : The entries in the parenthesis denote the number of pure tenants and those without are the number of owner-tenants.

large number of pure tenants as many as 38 are small tenants concentrated in the size group upto 3 acres. The owner-tenants preponderate in the size holdings of below 6 acres. There are some large pure tenants in the 12 acre and above size group, which is largely because in the villages of Attabira, Paramanpur and Babebira (in the Irrigated Region of Hirakund Dam Project) we find a number of large pure tenants who have migrated from Andhra Pradesh and are cultivating only leased in land.

We also notice from the sample a significant number of landlords belonging to small and medium size holdings respectively. Many of these landlords owning small holdings have leased out land to tenants with holdings (operational holdings) larger than the owned holdings of these small lessors. It may be roughly inferred that the tenants' status may not be far inferior to that of the small landlords. On the contrary, the big landlords appear to lease out in most cases to tenants with smaller operational holdings. These landlords may be said to be in a superior position vis-a-vis their tenants. Some tenants with operational holding larger than 12 acres lease in land from small and medium landlords and also from big landlords.[12]

The frequency distribution of lease units in lessor-lessee matrix might not give a complete picture of the lease market. Therefore, we have worked out the distribution of the lease area in a similar matrix form by lessor-lessee groups of different areas separately and for all the villages taken together, in order to study the lease pattern. Our findings so far as the distribution of the lease area is concerned, corroborate our conclusions drawn on the analysis of distribution of lease units. (See Table 3.4)

While big landlords lease out proportionately more land to the small and medium size tenants the small landlords lease out prominently to tenants operating in the medium size holdings only. The only exception is where a comparatively larger area is being leased out to tenants with operational holdings of more than 12 acres by lessors in the above 20 acre size class, in the irrigated

TABLE : 3.4

Distribution of Leased Area by Lessee-Lessor Groups—All Villages

Operational Holding of Tenants (Acres) \ *Ownership Holding of Landlords (Acres)*	*0-3*	*3-6*	*6-8*	*8-12*	*12-20*	*20+*	*Total (Area in Acres)*
0-3	9.38	12.88	13.66	12.42	25.40	5.10	78.84
3-6	25.50	27.28	10.69	10.58	23.50	19.95	117.50
6-8	8.70	8.30	20.70	3.40	7.50	13.00	61.60
8-12	2.50	4.00	-	-	19.50	4.00	30.00
12+	8.75	5.00	10.00	14.00	4.00	38.00	79.75
Total (Area in Acres)	54.83	57.46	55.05	40.40	79.90	80.05	367.69

region of Sambalpur district (villages of Attabira , Parmanpur and Babebira) for convenience we call it as Irrigated Region II and the irrigated village Lunahar we call it as Irrigated Region I. (Where big landlords have leased out in large parcels).

Consequently, among the lessees the amount of land leased in by small and medium class tenants is conspicuous. Particularly, the amount of land leased in by lessees in the category of 3-6 acres is quite prominent. The total area leased in by these two categories of tenants constitutes more than half of the total lease area. A sizeable proportion i.e. 22 per cent of the total lease area is leased in by the large tenants , operating in holdings of more than 12 acre size class. This arises predominantly because of the large leases in Irrigated Region II where we have a number of tenants who have migrated from Andhra Pradesh and have settled down here and have leased in large parcels of land. In fact, in the other villages under study, we do not find such large tenants.

1. Irrigated Villages

The lessee-lessor matrix of the irrigated villages (Table 3.5) shows a large number of pure tenants scattered in all size classes, many of these pure tenants are above 12 acres group conspicuously in the Irrigated Region of Attabira, Babebira, Parmanpur villages of the Sambalpur district. With the introduction of the HYV paddy cultivation, many such pure tenants have migrated from Andhra Pradesh and have temporarily settled in these villages of Irrigated Region II. In fact, there is a large influx of such tenant families in the district of Sambalpur who are spread over a large number of villages where cultivation of HYV paddy has been started following the introduction of irrigation facilities in the area in 60s. Some of these tenants operate large holdings of more than 12 acres in size. However, the majority of leases in both the Irrigated Regions are leased out by landlords owning above 8 acres of land and to tenants mostly with operational holdings of below 6 acres.

TABLE : 3.5

Frequency Distribution of Lease Units According to Lessee-Lessor Group—Irrigated Area

Operational Holding of Tenants (Acres) \ *Ownership Holding of Landlords (Acres)*	*0-3*	*3-6*	*6-8*	*8-12*	*12-20*	*20+*	*Total*
0-3	-	3	2	1	5	-	11
	(1)	(2)	(2)	(2)	-	-	(13)
3-6	1	1	-	1	2	1	6
	(5)	-	-	(1)	(2)	(3)	(11)
6-8	1	-	-	-	-	1	2
8-12	-	1	-	-	1	-	2
12+	1	-	-	-	1	-	2
	(3)	(1)	(3)	(1)	(2)	(3)	(13)
Total	3	5	2	2	9	2	23
	(9)	(3)	(5)	(4)	(10)	(6)	(37)

Note : Entries in the parenthesis denote the number of pure tenants and those without are the number of owner-tenants.

The reason as to why big landlords lease out to tenants with operational holdings of not very large size, may be due to the fact that owned holding of these tenants not being very large, it is presumed that these tenants would cultivate the land more intensively.[13] Consequently, the produce rents appropriated by landlords will be more, especially in the Irrigated Region I where land parcels are being leased out on a crop-sharing basis. In this region, ordinary varieties of paddy are being cultivated during the Kharif season while in Rabi season the HYV paddy is being cultivated. Unlike the *kharif* season, we find during the *rabi* season, tenants from the neighbouring villages to be leasing in land and cultivating the HYV paddy. These are tenants either with very small amount of owned land or with no land at all. Lack of irrigation facilities in the neighouring village is the major factor for which tenants come to this village to seek leases during the *rabi* season. Genrally, the lease is given on a crop sharing system. In the *kharif* season when ordinary paddy is grown the crop is shared on a 50/50 basis while in the *rabi* season when the HYV is grown the total produce is divided on a 25/75 basis, 25 per cent of the produce being appropriated by the landlord as rent. The landlord agrees to lease out on crop-sharing arrangement because even with this lower share, the landlords appear to be securing more amount of paddy as rent compared to that accruing in the *kharif* season, due to increase in production under HYV cultivation. Secondly, the pure and small owner-tenants migrating from the neighbouring villages reportedly take more interest and seem to make all possible endeavour to maximise the yield from this second crop.

On the contrary, we find that in the Irrigated Region II a significant proportion of the pure tenants of Andhra origin lease in large parcels of land and thus have larger operational holdings compared to the local tenants, largely because, these immigrant tenants have greater command over resources compared to the tenants of the village.

Unlike the Irrigated Region I, here in Region II, we find that big landlords do not show any particular preference for any particular types of tenants. Such an indifference is presumably because of the fact that rent is fixed and is being paid in advance in most cases of lease. The large tenants are seen to be leasing in from small as well as large landowners and thus dominating the lease market. Pure tenants are seen to be scattered in all size classes while owner-tenants are prominently noticeable in the small size class of less than 3 acres.

These remarks based on the frequency distribution of lease units are also corroborated by the distribution of the lease area. We find (See Table 3.6) some lessees in the size group of above 12 acre holding, lease in a sizeable area. On the other hand, small and medium class lessees of less than 6 acres lease in a significant proportion of the total lease area, leasing in prominently from lessors with holding of more than 12 acres.

The maximum amount of land is leased out by lessors in the size class of 20 acres and above, followed by the lessors in the 12-20 acre size class. But the amount of land leased out by lessors below 6 acres of holding is significant.

2. Unirrigated Villages

The situation is different in the unirrigated villages, where pure tenants are fewer. (See Table 3.7) The owner-tenants are concentrated in 3-6 acre size group. The small landowners lease out to tenants who economically seem to be better off and operate on holdings which are larger compared to their (lessors') ownership holdings. This may be due to the fact that the small landowners do not find it economically worthwhile to undertake self-cultivation in the tiny parcels of land they own. Moreover, access to credit market being limited, and their own resources being scarce, these very small landowners are not in a position to lease in land in order to make their operational holding a viable cultivating unit.

TABLE : 3.6

Distribution of Leased area by Lessee-Lessor Groups—Irrigated Area

Operational Holding of Tenants (Acres) \ Ownership Holding of Landlords (Acres)	0-3	3-6	6-8	8-12	12-20	20+	Total (Area in Acres)
0-3	2.00	6.48	3.02	2.52	13.50	-	27.52
3-6	8.80	-	-	.50	8.50	11.00	28.80
6-8	-	-	-	-	1.50	2.50	4.00
8-12	1.00	4.00	-	-	4.00	-	9.00
12+	6.00	5.00	10.00	4.00	4.00	38.00	67.00
Total (Area in Acres)	17.80	15.48	13.02	7.02	31.50	51.50	136.32

TABLE : 3.7

Frequency Distribution of Lease Units According to Lessee - Lessor Groups—Unirrigated Area

Operational Holding of Tenants (Acres) \ *Ownership holding of Landlords (Acres)*	*0-3*	*3-6*	*6-8*	*8-12*	*12-20*	*20+*	*Total*
0-3	-	-	-	2	1	1	4
	-	(1)	(1)	-	(1)	-	(3)
3-6	11	8	7	2	4	1	33
	-	(1)	-	-	(2)	-	(3)
6-8	3	4	3	1	1	-	12
8-12	-	-	-	-	1	2	3
12+	2	-	-	1	-	-	3
Total	16	12	10	6	7	4	55
	-	(2)	(1)	-	(3)	-	(6)

Note : Entries in the parenthesis denote the member of pure tenants and those without the member of owner-tenants.

TABLE : 3.8

Distribution of Leased Area by Lessee-Lessor Groups—Unirrigated Area

Operational Holding of Tenants (Acres) \ *Ownership Holding of Landlords (Acres)*	*0-3*	*3-6*	*6-8*	*8-12*	*12-20*	*20+*	*Total (Area in Acres)*
0-3	-	3.00	.24	2.00	3.50	1.00	9.74
3-6	6.90	11.10	5.64	2.78	11.00	.70	38.12
6-8	1.00	5.20	7.30	1.00	2.00	3.00	19.50
8-12	-	-	-	-	2.00	2.00	4.00
12+	2.75	-	-	10.00	-	-	12.75
Total (Area in Acres)	10.65	19.30	13.18	15.78	18.50	6.70	84.11

Cultivation of crop largely depends upon the monsoon which is very uncertain. Therefore, not being assured of crop, the small landowners shirk the risk of cultivation and instead lease out the land to comparatively better off farmers.

Among the lesses, it is noticed that pure tenatns are few. The owner-tenants in the size group 3-6 acres are seen to be the most effective lessees and conspicuous in the lease market by leasing in the maximum number of lease units.

We note a similar situation when we look at the distribution of lease area (See Table 3.8). We find that tenants with medium size class operational holding predominate the lease market by leasing in the maximum amount of land. Lessors of all categories lease out mostly to the lessees operating medium size holding which is evident in the matrix. The mode size of tenants operational holding in this region is larger than that in the irrigated region as a whole although smaller than that in the Irrigated Region II taken separately.

3. Cash Crop Area

In the cash crop area, we do not find many lessors in the small size holdings (See Table 3.9). The lessors are mostly clustered between 3-12 acre size class. In fact, there is only one in the below 3 acres holdings and none above 20 acre size class. There are many lessors who are Brahmin by caste and do not undertake self-cultivation because of caste inhibitions and consequently lease out the entire land they own.

We find in the lessee-lessor matrix big landowners leasing out land to small pure tenatns and owner-tenants operating mostly on less than 6 acre size holdings. In all, out of 44 lease units in the cash crop area 30 units have been leased out to owner-tenants while the remaining 14 have been leased out to pure tenants.

The distribution of leased area (Table 3.10) shows that maximum amount of land is leased out to small and medium class tenants and among them they lease in a little more than two-thirds of the total lease area.

TABLE : 3.9

Frequency Distribution of Lease Units by Lessee-Lessor Groups—Cash Crop Area

Operational Holding of Tenants (Acres) \ *Ownership Holding of Landlords (Acres)*	*0-3*	*3-6*	*6-8*	*8-12*	*12-20*	*20+*	*Total*
0-3	-	3	5	1	2	-	11
	-	(1)	(4)	(4)	(2)	-	(11)
3-6	-	7	4	3	-	-	14
	-	-	(2)	-	-	-	(2)
6-8	1	1	2	1	-	-	5
	-	-	(1)	-	-	-	(1)
8-12	-	-	-	-	-	-	-
12+	-	-	-	-	-	-	-
Total	1	11	11	5	2	-	30
	-	(1)	(7)	(4)	(2)	-	(14)

Note : Entries in the parenthesis denote the number of pure tenants and those without are the member of owner-tenants.

TABLE : 3.10

Distribution of Leased Area by Lessee-Lessor Groups—Cash Crop Area

Ownership Holding of Landlords (Acres) / *Operational Holding of Tenants (Acres)*	*0-3*	*3-6*	*6-8*	*8-12*	*12-20*	*20+*	*Total (Area in Acres)*
0-3	-	3.40	10.40	6.90	6.20	-	20.90
3-6	-	7.18	5.05	7.30	-	3.25	22.78
6-8	0.20	0.60	11.40	2.40	-	-	14.60
8-12	-	-	-	-	-	-	-
12+	-	-	-	-	-	-	-
Total (Area in Acres)	0.20	11.18	26.85	16.60	6.20	3.25	64.28

4. Tribal Area

A peculiar distribution of the lease units is noticed in the tribal villages (See Table 3.11). There are a large number of lessors in the below 6 acre size class and then a number of them in the above 12 acre size class but none is seen in between. The number of small landlords is quite significant.

Both small as well as big landowners lease out to tenants dispersed in all size classes but more prominently to small tenants. In general, there appears to be a preference for the owner-tenants by lessors of both categories so that among the lessees in all categories, one finds the existence of larger number of owner-tenants.

The distribution pattern of the lease area show (Table - 3.12) that a sizeable land is being leased in by tenants in the medium size group. Among the lessors in this region, we note that the maximum amount of area, constituting a little less than one-third of the total is being leased out by lessors in the small size class. Both small as well as big landowners lease out prominently to tenants operating in medium size holdings.

We may now briefly summarise the salient features of the lease patterns observed in the different regions under study. In the lease market, there exist, on the one hand, the big landlords who supply a large proportion of the lease area and thus predominate the supply side of the lease market. These landowners lease out mostly to small and medium class (both in pure and owner-tenants categories) preferably to small lessees. On the other hand, we also find lessors who are small landowners and are quite significant both numerically and by the proportion of land they lease out. Lessors of the latter category seem to have no specific preference for tenants of particular types except that they lease out to medium size tenants with relatively better economic position than that of their own.

On the demand side, we note that the significant categories

TABLE 3.11

Frequency Distribution of Lease by Lessee-Lessor Groups—Tribal Area

Operational Holding of Tenants (Acres) \ Ownership Holding of Landlords (Acres)	0-3	3-6	6-8	8-12	12-20	20+	Total
0-3	7	2	-	-	2	4	15
	(7)	-	-	-	(1)	(3)	(11)
3-6	5	5	-	-	1	3	14
6-8	5	2	-	-	-	2	9
	(2)	-	-	-	(1)	(1)	(4)
8-12	2	-	-	-	-	1	3
12+	-	-	-	-	1	-	1
Total	19	9	-	-	4	10	42
	(9)	-	-	-	(2)	(4)	(15)

TABLE : 3.12

Distribution of Leased Area by Lessee-Lessor Groups—Tribal Area

Operational Holding of Tenants (Acres) \ *Ownership Holding of Landlords (Acres)*	*0-3*	*3-6*	*6-8*	*8-12*	*12-20*	*20+*	*Total (Area in Acres)*
0-3	7.38	-	-	1.00	2.20	4.10	14.68
3-6	9.80	9.00	-	-	4.00	5.00	27.80
6-8	7.50	2.50	-	-	4.00	7.50	21.50
8-12	1.50	-	-	-	13.50	2.00	17.00
12+	-	-	-	-	-	-	-
Total (Area in Acres)	26.18	11.50	-	1.00	23.70	18.60	80.98

of lessees in the lease markets are pure and owner-tenants in the small and medium size holdings. Owner-tenants in the medium size holdings seem to be preferred and are seen to be leasing in from the big as well as small landlords (who show preference for owne-tenants even to a greater degree) and therefore, dominating the lease market as a whole. In fact out of the 222 lease units in our sample villages, 150 units have been leased out to owner-tenants who own some amount of land. Medium class owner-tenants have proved to be most effective lessees in the lease market followed by small pure tenants. Area-wise we find it is the tenants in the 3-6 acre size holdings have leased in almost one-third of the total lease area.

Depending upon the respective social and agro-economic conditions prevailing in the different areas, landlords and tenants show different behaviour. To take the villages in Irrigated Region I, we find, on the whole, the big landlords leasing out prominently to small pure and owner-tenants, which suggests that landowners in the irrigated area prefer to lease out land to pure and owner-tenants having very small owned holdings. In the irrigated villages, we also find very small landowners leasing out. It is explicit from the lessor-lessee matrix (Irrigated Area) that such landlords have leased out largely to medium class tenants in the 3-6 acre size group , i.e., lessees with some amount of owned land and having operational holding which is usually larger than the ownership holding of the lessors. In Irrigated Region II, we find some lessees operating with large tenanted holding which may be due to landlords' indifference in selection of tenants because land parcels are leased out on fixed rents, though the big landlords continue to express generally their preference for leasing out in small parcels, the size distribution of actual parcels in the region show that there are few large ones.

The unirrigated areas, however, show certain different features. Unlike the irrigated villages, we find that big landlords with more than 12 acre holdings appear to prefer leasing out to owner-tenants operating with medium size holdings.

Similar is the case with small landowners who show a similar preference to lease out to owner-tenants with medium size operational holding. In fact, not a single pure tenant is seen to have taken any lease from landlords with below 3 acres of holding. Thus, the owner-tenants in the medium size class are seen to be dominating the lease market and have been most effective as lessees.

A similar situation appears to prevail in the cash crop area where owner-tenants seem to be dominating the lease market and the lessors showing an inclination to lease out to small and medium class tenants.

In the tribal areas, again, we find owner-tenants in the different size classes to be dominating both numerically and area wise. Here, too, we find that small and medium owner-tenants are prominent. The small landowners also show a similar preference to lease out to owner-tenants.

Thus, probing into the question as to who leases from whom we have seen here how the initial resource position of the tenants influences the lease market and determines as to how far effective he would be as lessee in the lease market. While leasing out, the initial resource position of the tenant is, no doubt the major consideration for landlords particularly the large landowners. The small landowners, however, do not show any specific choice while leasing out, but usually, they are seen to be leasing out to tenants who have better resource position than their own. All these, as we have noted in above discussion have a great impact on the lease pattern. But it will be more revealing to see how various other factors are also taken into consideration by lessors while leasing out. These, too, influence significantly the lease market and the agrarian relations. In the following chapter, we will discuss the different factors motivating landlords of various classes while leasing out to particular type of tenants.

REFERENCES

1. For Orissa, there are certain inter-distict differences, but the broad picture remains almost same.
2. G. Dash, "Tenancy Reforms in Orissa: Its Impact and Policy Option", paper presented in the workshop on Land Reforms, Bhubaneswar, Feb.'93.
3. "Among those who lease in though landless marginal and small farmers constituted a sizable majority, semi-medium, medium and large farmers were not insignificant." G. Dash, *Ibid.*
4. *Studies of the Economics of Farm Management, Cuttack District.* (Unpublished); and *Studies in the Economics of Farm Management, Sambalpur District*, Ministry of Food and Agriculture, New Delhi.
   The data of the Farm management studies are not adequate nor comprehensive. The main purpose of the Farm Management Studies was to study the nature of operations and the input output relationship of different farms. Therefore, for our purpose, it has certain limitations e.g. the date do not give any importance to tenurial contracts etc. However, we have made use of the data in order to draw certain suggestive inferences.
5. See Table III (A) - III (B), (24 and 259 st. level), *Report on Agricultural Census of Orissa* 1970-71. (Board of Revenue, Government of Orissa, 1975).
6. "...The landholding survey brings out a convincing downward trend, as holding size increases in proportion of leased in area to total area operated, quite contrary to what has been observed by Khusro. Up to 2.50 acres the leased in area generally exceeds the owned area. Although a substantial proportion is leased in by holding (Mixed) in all size groups, the proportion decreases over the scale of holding size and owned area remains the more important factor." S.K. Sanyal, "Size holdings and some factor related to production", *Economic and Political Weekly*, (16 August 1969), pp. 1, 345-46.
7. V.M. Rao, "Village Lease Markets for Agricultural Land; Some approaches for analysis", *Economic and Political Weekly*, Review of Agriculture (June 1974), pp. 55-62.
8. Some of the findings of our study particularly relating to lease patterns and tenurial conditions prevailing in some selected

villages of Orissa have been presented earlier in two articles - See "Tenurial Conditions and Mode of Exploitation — A Study of Some villages in Orissa" *Economic and Political Weekly*, (Annual Number, February, 1975), pp. 221-40; and "Tenurial Conditions and Mode of Exploitations: Study of Some villages in Orissa — Some Further Notes", *Economic and Political Weekly* (Review of Agriculture, June 21-28), pp. A 49-55.

9. See discussion in Chapter 2.
10. There has been a re-organisation of the districts of Orissa in the recent years. So, the names of the districts mentioned here should be treated as districts as they existed prior to the re-organisation.
11. To cite but an example, in our sample, there is a landlord in one of the tribal villages of Phulbani, who owns a small grocery shop and sells mostly to villagers. He expects his tenants to purchase from him and if he would have more number of tenants then his sales would increase. Sometimes, he sells the commodities on credit, rather he induces his tenants to buy things and pay later, so that the tenants will be bound to remain indebted to him perpetually because in most cases these tenants will not be in a position to repay the loan, and they remain indebted to the landlord and therefore have to abide by all the terms and conditions of lease as laid down by the landlord.
12. One of the purposes we have in mind in detailing *who lessees from whom* it to confront the relative economic status of the landlord and his tenant. While data concerning size of holding is relatively easily available that concerning ownership of other assets, income from other sources, etc., is rather difficult to obtain. Ideally, speaking the economic status should have been represented by a comprehensive index of resource position of individual households. Even this would not be adequate considering that ownership of land may bestow economic status and power beyond the financial value of land owned. To supplement the information on holdings, we therefore, worked out for each size-category of landlord and tenant household a representative value for annual net income from all sources (Table 3.9). The figures are admittedly crude and are at best only indicative. On the basis of these admittedly crude and partial data, we may say that the economic status of the middle tenants is not much inferior to that to the small landlords.

13. "It is presumed that these lessees would cultivate the land more intensively because of economic necessity by using both labour and non-labour resources particularly more of family labour far beyond the point of maximum net return. The landlord so parcelling out land may be in a position to extract a maximum rent." — Krishna Bharadwaj, *Production Conditions in Indian Agriculture*, Cambridge, 1974, p. 4.

4

LEASING-IN AND LEASING-OUT — SOME MOTIVATIONAL FACTORS

Consideration which influence leasing out and leasing-in of land are largely determined by the resource position and the socio-economic status of both the landlords and the tenants participating in the lease market.

In the preceding chapter, we have noticed some peculiar characteristics of the lease market and how the relative economic position of landlords *vis-a-vis* tenants influence the lease pattern. Landlords appear to show preferences for particular types of tenants while leasing-out land. We have seen such preferences to be varying in different regions depending upon the prevailing agricultural situation and infrastructure available in the area. While landlords in the irrigated region appear to reveal a preference for leasing-out to tenants who do not own land or operate small sized holdings, in other areas, landlords seem to prefer to lease out to tenants owning small amount of land and operating medium size holdings between 3-6 acres.

Tenants operating with holdings between 3-6 acres have proved to be the most effective lessees by leasing in the maximum amount of land out of the total area leased out. In addition to the particular preference of landlords for tenants with some (but not substantial) owned land, the better economic status of this class of owner-tenants have enabled them to be more prominent in the lease market. The basic considerations which determine leasing out of land could be broadly classified into two groups — one, the economic consideration and second, the social relations i.e. the status enjoyed by landowners in the village. The need for the latter consideration arises in our case particularly because our sample villages are mostly from the *zamindari* tracts where lessors belong the traditional landlord class. Or, as seen in our sample village Nalabanta, where mainly cash crop is produced, the lessors, mostly *Brahmin* by caste, consider self-cultivation as undermining their status and, therefore, they do not undertake self-cultivation. Apart from the above two considerations there is a third category of reasons for leasing out i.e. lessors leasing out because of their physical inability. The last may arise in the case, for example, of either a child or widow landowner. We may also include in this category families who do not have manpower to undertake self-cultivation. In the category of land owners who are leasing out because of economic consideration we may include some landlords who suffer from lack of economic resources in order to hire labour and non-labour resources to carry out self-cultivation. Lack of accessibility to credit and other factor market hinders this class of landowners from obtaining credit and other factor inputs. The particular holding might be a tiny one and it may not be worthwhile to undertake self-cultivation. The same factor may also inhibit leasing in land to supplement the ownership holding. Therefore, under these circumstances, they may opt for leasing out the land. This category of lessors may be classified as landlords leasing out under distress conditions. Contrary to this we find large land owners who lease out land not because they are incapable of cultivating it by themselves but because they find it economic to lease out since it ensures a flow of regular income without necessarily having to share any cost of cultivation. Thus we find simultaneous existence of various considerations under which landlords lease out.

We have covered in all 80 landlords from the different

TABLE : 4.1

Reasons for Leasing-Out : Frequency of Responses

	Irrigated Area	*Unirrigated Area*	*Cash Crop Area*	*Tribal Area*	*Total*
"The plot is away from residence"	-	1	2	-	3
"No farming experience"	-	-	-	2	2
"Physically handicap"*	1	1	1	2	5
"Traditionally a landlord"**	8	17	20	2	47
"More lucrative to lease out"	6	2	1	1	10
"Not having sufficient manpower in family"	2	4	2	8	16
"Financial difficulty to carry out self-cultivation"	1	1	-	4	6
"Other reasons"	-	4***	3***	1***	8
No response -	-	-	1	1	2
Total Responses	18	30	30	21	99

* In the cases recorded here either a widow or a child was the owner.

** This was mainly associated with caste.

*** Engaged in business of other services.

villages belonging to the different areas; 17 from the irrigated villages, 22 from villages with no irrigation facilities, 25 from the villages producing cash crops and 16 from tribal villages.

Reasons for Leasing Out

We have enquired through questionnaire into various possible factors motivating the leasing out of land. The different considerations determining the lease have been grouped under various heads. The responses to the questionnaire are quite revealing. We have also enquired into questions such as, what sort of tenants the lessors would prefer while leasing out, the responses to which divulge different preferences. The lessors have also shown their preference for leasing out land in parcels of particular sizes. Since landlords stated in their replies various reasons for their leasing out land, in many cases we have recorded more than one reason stated by the respondents. Therefore, the number of responses recorded here (Table 4.1) exceeds the total number of respondents. Only two lessors, one each from cash crop and tribal areas could not cite any reason in particular. We present below the various reasons stated by landlords.

(i) *The Plot is Away from Residence*: Not many landlords have reported this to be the major factor responsible for their leasing out. There are only two such cases in cash crop area and one in the unirrigated area. Therefore, this does not appear to constitute a major reason for leasing out in our survey.

(ii) *No Farming Experience*: This too is rarely seen to be the only factor for a lessor to lease out land. Only in the tribal area there are two landlords who have stated this as a factor responsible for leasing out land.

(iii) *Physically Handicapped:* Out of 99 responses, there are only five where this has been stated as a major factor. In the irrigated area we found an old lady, whose son is in service elsewhere and who, therefore, is leasing out. Similarly in the cash crop area, the lessor is an old lady who does not have anybody to look after the land and therefore, leases out on fixed cash rent. In the unirrigated and tribal areas as well those who have cited this as a reason are old persons.

(iv) *Traditionally Landlord:* In fact the majority of the responses cluster in this category. We have stated earlier that our villages mostly belong to the *zamindari* tracts of the state and it is largely because of this reason that we find a majority of landlords have stated this to be predominately responsible for leasing out land. Out of the total 99 responses, 47 belong to this category of traditional landlords. In cash crop area, most of the lessors are Brahmins who do not undertake personal cultivation due to religious inhibitions and fear that self-cultivation would undermine their social status. Out of the 30 responses there, 20 belong to this category and have reported themselves to be 'traditional landlords'. In unirrigated villages we also find a similar class of traditional landlords to be dominating.

(v) *More Lucrative to Lease-Out:* Such a response is significant because of the fact that landlords leasing out under this consideration have a well-defined 'economic' point of view. In irrigated areas, especially in Irrigated Region II, landlords find leasing out to be convenient and lucrative too. In this region lessors are more interested in fixed cash rent and lease out only for a short duration so that rent thereof can be further increased in successive leases. Landlords belonging to this category are generally large landowners, and they lease out in small parcels to a large number of tenants. These landlords lease out not because of scare resources or lack of manpower or because of the difficulty that their landholding is an uneconomic unit for cultivation but because it ensures a regular source of income without having to shoulder any responsibility of cultivation. This class of landlords do not share any production costs either, unless it is worthwhile to do so (such is the case of Irrigated Region I where the landlords share a part of the fertiliser cost in order to induce the tenant farmers to produce more).

(vi) *Not Having Sufficient Manpower in the Family:* This is seen more in unirrigated villages and in tribal areas. Due to lack of adequate number of working members in the families, these families have been compelled to lease out the entire amount of land that they possess. More often than not, most of the families also lack sufficient resources to hire labour services to supplement their family labour to carry out cultivation. Thus we find, lack of sufficient working members in the family coupled with limited investable resources compel families of this category to lease out land and seek employment elsewhere. In irrigated and cash crop areas we find there also exist such kind of lessors. In these areas, particularly because of huge labour input requirements during different periods of cultivation, it becomes difficult for a cultivating household to rely on its own family labour. Therefore, in spite of the attraction of a good yield, some of these landowners in the irrigated areas are compelled to lease out.

(vii) *Financial Difficulties to Carry Out Self-Cultivation:* We have just indicated how lack of financial resources is a major factor for small landowners to lease out land even though they are interested in cultivating their own land personally. In the tribal areas particularly we find a large number of lessors belong to this category.

(viii) *Other Reasons:* This category includes lessors who are engaged either in service or business and lease out since they are preoccupied otherwise.

Thus while a majority of landowners have given 'being traditional landlords' as the reason for leasing out, it is significant to find that in irrigated and tribal areas economic considerations appear to weigh more than elsewhere. In the former category we find landlords mostly belonging to higher castes or landlords belonging to the old *zamindari* tracts where as in the latter category we have landlords who lease out mainly because it is lucrative and convenient to do so. This is because the rent earned is considerable, convenient and regular. However, both categories of landlords (traditional as well as those leasing out because it is convenient to do so) can be grouped as a class of sleeping partners in the production process since they do not share any production responsibility.

Pecuniary stringencies accompanied with inaccessibility to the credit markets (which again depends upon the tangible assets that one owns) restrict some of the small landowners from going for self-cultivation. In irrigated and cash crop areas there are agencies (mainly service cooperatives) which provide credit to the interested farmers. Since in these areas the tenants either produce cash crops or high yielding varieties of paddy, they take the risk of incurring credits because they can repay it after the harvest. But in unirrigated and tribal villages crops are not assured and therefore, tenants or small farmers find it difficult to obtain loans or hesitate to borrow since they may not be able to repay the same. Moreover, in these areas loans from cooperative society and from government sources being rare, private agencies (who supply credit) charge exorbitant rates of interest. Very often loans are advanced against land or such other tangible property. The only source from which these loans could be repaid is the annual harvest. But since crops are not assured there is always the fear of losing land or such other properties mortgaged against the loan. Consequently, these small landowners prefer to lease out not because they want to live as rentiers, but because major risk is involved in undertaking self-cultivation.

Preference for Particular Types of Tenants

The landlords show particular preference while choosing their tenants. In order to know the particular preference of lessors we have divided tenants into different categories — labourers, pure tenants, owner-tenants i.e. tenants who own some amount of land, and any other type apart from these three. We have further classified the tenants in the pure and owner-tenant categories into differents groups according to their operational holdings: Small tenants operating in the below 3 acres holdings, medium size tenants operating in the 3 to 8 acre size land holdings, and big with more than 8 acres of operational holdings. The frequency of responses expressing preference for tenants are more than the number of lessors since the lessors have showen the order of preference for tenants of different types. (See Table 4.2).

Generally the owner-tenants are seen to be preferred to pure tenants, and very often it is the operational holding of a tenant, which appears to be the main consideration of lessors while leasing out land. We find, that pure tenants with medium size operational holding and owner-tenants with a small sized owned holding are mostly preferred. The reason largely is the presumption of lessors that such tenants with operational holding of medium size would confine their whole interest only to agriculture where as in case of very big owner-tenants it is presumed that they would take more interest in the owned land rather than in the leased in land. Therefore, we find, owner-tenants with small owned holdings are preferred by lessors. When the leased in land constitutes a major portion of the operational holding it is expected that the tenant will pay more attention to the leased in area and it would be more paying for a lessor under the share-cropping system of land tenure. In fact we enquired from the tenants if they discriminate between the owned land and the leased in land (if cultivating both simultaneously). The response was revealing. While those with substantial holding were either indifferent or preferred to invest on their owned land, those with meagre land of their own preferred to work more intensively on the leased in land. This they attributed to the insecurity of lease otherwise. Further, the preference for

TABLE : 4.2

Frequency of Responses Expressing Preference for Tenant

Preference in Favour of	*Irrigated Area*	*Unirrigated Area*	*Cash Crop Area*	*Tribal Area*	*Total*
Labourers	1*	-	1*	1*	3
Pure Tenants					
Small (upto 3 acres)	1	-	5	1	7
Medium (3 to 8 acres)	11	21	13	11	56
Big (above 8 acres)	-	-	-	-	-
Owner-Tenants					
Small (upto 3 acres)	12	18	15	10	55
Medium (3 to 8 acres)	2	3	7	2	14
Big (above 8 acres)	-	-	-	-	-
Any Other Stipulation	2**	1***	1***	1***	5
No Response	-	2	-	-	2
Total	29	45	42	26	152

* 'Should possess a plough'.

** The replies were: (i) 'those who pay rent regularly', (ii) 'my own caste ('*teli*').

*** 'Family with a bullock'.

middle size tenants of the pure category is supported by the argument that such tenants may have resources of their own which the small pure tenants might not have. Therefore, pure tenants with some amount of land already leased in and owner-tenants with small amount of owned land are preferred to tenants with larger owned holdings. This, however, does not contradict our earlier statement that middle size owner tenants are seen to be predominant since there we have referred to operational holding of the owner-tenants where as here we have referred to the ownership holdings of the owner-tenants. In the matrix showing (See Table 4.3) owned holdings of both landlords and tenants, tenants with small owned holdings predominate among the lessees especially those leasing in from large landowners.

We also find some lessors who prefer to lease out to labourers, but it is always accompanied with the condition that the labourer must own a plough and must have sufficient manpower in the family. Both these factors are determinants of potential labour effort of a tenant family. In response to our query lessors have stated that while leasing out they consider the number of working members of the tenant family and their efficiency.[1] Generally larger families appear to put in more of family labour because of economic necessity.

Size of Lease Parcels

We have also noted landlords showing preference to leasing out in different size parcels. Most of the landlords prefer to lease out in small parcels. The reason advanced was that output obtainable would be higher as tenant families work harder on smaller farms. Such a preference exists in all sample villages particularly in village Lunahar in our Irrigated Region I whereas in the Irrigated Region II some lessors lease out land in large parcels. In the former case the primary consideration is that a small operational holding induces the tenant farmer to put in more of

TABLE : 4.3

Frequency of Lease Units by Lessee - Lessor Groups—All Villages

Owned Holding of Tenants \ *Owned Holding of Landlords*	*0-3*	*3-6*	*6-8*	*8-12*	*12-20*	*20+*	*Total*
3	29	27	21	11	20	12	120
3-6	8	9	2	1	1	4	25
6-8	1	-	-	-	1	-	2
8-12	-	-	-	-	-	-	-
12+	2	-	-	1	-	-	3
Total	40	36	23	13	22	16	150

labour and other inputs because they can raise more output (even though the total produce is shared between him and the lessor). Similarly lessors presume that these tenants would cultivate the leased in land more intensively and consequently their (lessors') share would increase (since rent is a proportion of the total produce the rental amount would increase when the total produce increases). In the case of the Irrigated Region II, where lease parcels are generally large in size, lease is given on a fixed rent basis. Therefore, the lessors lease out generally to those who offer the sum demanded. Thus under the crop sharing system of tenancy we find lessors are more cautious while leasing out than the lessors in areas where land is leased out on a fixed rent basis. In both these cases however, lessors appear to show their main concern over the amount of rent that would accrue to them, and accordingly they choose their tenants under different systems of land tenure, and decide in what parcels land should be leased out.

The consideration in unirrigated areas is however, different. In these villages we find lessors leasing out land in somewhat bigger parcels which may be presumably because very small parcels in these areas are not economically viable units. Thus a larger operational holding may be more economical to the lessor. In tribal area while bigger landlords reportedly show a preference to lease out in small parcels and to a large number of tenants, majority have no particular preference to express possibly because of the predominance of small landlords for whom the question is not very relevant.

To sum up, we have noted that considerations like the lessors' preference for particular type of lessees and choice to lease out land in particular size parcels, no doubt have a great impact on the structure and behaviour of the lease market. In the villages under study we find generally the owner-tenants are preferred to pure tenants (who had already some land leased in) and the latter in turn to labourers. It is also interesting to note the reasons advanced for particular preference. We notice a landlord while prepared to lease out to a labourer insists that the labourer must have a plough and must have sufficient manpower in the family to work in the field. The preference for middle size lessees in the pure tenant category is supported by the argument that such a tenant may have resources of his own which a small pure tenant may not have. Among the owner-tenants preference is particularly shown for those with small owned holdings because owner-tenants with a larger proportion of owned land in the operational holding might neglect the leased in parcels and take more care of the owned land. We have seen lessors invariably preferring tenants with families having efficient working members, tenants with some amount of owned or leased in land and possessing some non-labour resources investible in land.

All these considerations no doubt significantly influence the landlord-tenant nexus. While the initial resource position of the tenant and the landlord more or less determines the lease pattern, it also forms the basis of determining the lease terms and conditions.

REFERENCES

1. To cite, but one instance - in the village Balrampur there lives a tenant who has two sons, one of whom works in the field, helps his father in cultivation. In the village the farmer and his son both are considered to be very efficient. Therefore, in spite of the fact that he owns a tiny parcel of land, he is the most sought after tenant. Indeed he refuses to take all offers of leases and accepts only a few because he thinks that beyond a point the operational unit cannot be extended. Thus in some cases it is the efficiency of the tenant family which becomes a major consideration for lessors while leasing out land.

5

TERMS AND CONDITIONS OF LEASE

In the present chapter, we will discuss how under seemingly identical tenurial systems, the terms and conditions change depending upon the relative resource position of the lessors and lessees. We have indicated in the preceding chapters that lessors and lessees are widely scattered in terms of their size of ownership and operational holdings respectively and have noticed that not all lessors are economically better off nor all tenants are economically worse in terms of their relative socio-economic status. We have also noted some important factors influencing motivations for leasing out. In some cases we have also noticed lessors being incapable of pursuing self-cultivation (either because of lack of work force within the family or lack of economic means to afford various inputs necessary to undertake self-cultivation) and therefore, leasing out 'under distress conditions'. Contrary to this we notice lessors who lease out under completely different circumstances. Unlike the former this class of lessors are large landowners and are capable of under taking self-cultivation. But instead they lease out because it is considered to be more lucrative. Thus both classes of lessors lease out because of economic reasons though the reasons are entirely different for the two groups of lessors. Another feature of the lease market which needs to be mentioned here is that small landowners while leasing out do not show any particular preference for specific type of tenants, whereas the large landowners prefer to lease out particularly to small and medium class tenants both in the pure and owner-tenant categories. Similarly among the lessees we find though they are spread over in all size classes, the most effective lessees have been the owner-tenants operating in the medium size holdings (3-8 acres holding). All these profoundly influence the lease pattern and the terms and conditions of the leases as well. The relative resource strength and the motivational factors largely determine the terms and conditions of each lease. We will discuss below how the terms and conditions are governed by the economic status of the lessors and lessees as indicated by the size of their ownership and operational holdings respectively.

We have collected information from lessees and their corresponding landlords in order to cross check the responses given by either. These information relate to the amount of land leased in from each landlord, the conditions accompanying each lease and the resource status of each lessor. All these will indicate how a particular tenant is treated differently by different landlords (depending upon the socio-economic status of both the land-owner and the tenant). The discussions below will show the different lease conditions persisting even under identical tenurial systems. At the first instance, we would restrict our discussions to the terms and conditions governing the principal crop—paddy or cash crop, as the case may be—cultivated under the different land tenure arrangements, whether crop sharing or fixed rent tenancy, and other conditions of lease like sharing of minor crops, by products, sharing of costs of production, rendering unpaid labour services etc. Our discussion will be based on our findings of the two surveys—first relating to survey in 1974-75 and second in the 90s. During the second survey in the 90s we could survey the same households (barring a few) which were covered during the

TABLE : 5.1 A

Unirrigrated Aea : Village — Bhaliamunda

*Sl. No. of Tenant**	*Tenant's Operational Holding (Acres)*	*Landlord's Ownership Holding (Acres)*	*Size of Leased Parcels (Acres)*	*Rents Per Acre (Quintals)*			*Rent as a Proportion of Output (Per cent)*
				Under Share-Cropping	*Under Fixed Kind*	*Converted Form Fixed Cash*	
1	2	3	4	5	6	7	8
1	4.00	13.00	3.00	-	2.50	-	39
2	3.00	5.00	3.00	-	1.83	-	47
3 a	4.00	16.00	2.00	-	2.00	-	36
b	-	5.00	1.00	-	1.50	-	44
c	-	13.00	1.00	-	2.50	-	36
4 a	5.00	16.00	2.50	-	2.50	-	45
b	-	4.00	0.50	-	2.00	-	45
5 a	8.50	4.00	2.00	-	1.50	-	48
b	-	16.00	2.00	-	2.00	-	44
c	-	4.00	1.00	-	1.50	-	46
6	3.00	16.00	2.00	-	2.00	-	45
7	1.50	16.00	1.50	-	2.00	-	43
8	8.00	30.00	3.00	-	2.66	-	43
9	22.00	10.00	10.00	-	-	0.61	17
10	4.40	4.00	3.00	3.33	-	-	50

*When the tenant has more than one lease, the lease units are recorded separately, with alphabetes following the serial number of the tenants.

first survey in mid 70s. The transition over the period is quite revealing and again shows how with changes in technology, availability of inputs like irrigation brings in complete shift in lease terms and condition. In all the sample villages except villages in tribal areas the changes are quite significant.

SECTION I

Lease Terms for the Principal Crop — (Area Wise)

Unirrigated Area : As stated earlier we have in our sample village Bhalliamunda, from the western part of the state and the other village Balarampur from the coastal region. In both the villages paddy is the only crop cultivated on the leased in lands. While in the village Bhaliamunda rent is generally paid in fixed kind, in Balarampur village rent constitutes a proportion of the total gross produce (a system of crop sharing tenancy).

Table 5.1A presents the figures for the village Bhalliamunda. We notice that barring only one case the rest pay fixed rents. Of those who pay fixed rents, one tenant pays fixed cash rent — the only case where the rent paid is unusually lower than the prevailing rent in the village. In this case the rent was advanced in cash to the lessor who was badly in need of money. In all other cases the rent is paid generally after the harvest. The per acre fixed rent varies from lease to lease and it may be observed here that the rent paid generally is higher in case of the tenants leasing in land from landlords who are economically better off. We have worked out the rent as a proportion of gross output which works out to be less than 50 per cent. In all cases tenants pay either in fixed cash or kind rents, whether paid prior to harvest or after it. In the single case where land is leased in on share-cropping basis the proportion of rent constitutes 50 per cent of the gross produce.

Fixed kind rent is of recent origin. In a few cases the

older tenants cultivating under share-cropping system have been evicted after the tenant declined to pay the higher rent demanded by the lessor. The tenant has been replaced by another who pays fixed rent. The fixed rent varies from 1.5 quintals to 2.66 quintals and again this has been increased recently.

In the village Balarampur, leases are generally given on a cropsharing basis. In our sample there is only one case where rent is fixed and paid in kind. But during the summer season some of the tenants of the village lease in plots of land from a neighbouring village where perennial canal water is available and high yielding variety (HYV) of paddy is cultivated. But while the conventional share of the landlord for ordinary paddy is 50 per cent of the gross produce, it is 25 per cent in the case of HYV paddy grown in the summer (See Table 5.1 B). We have worked out the actual rent paid by the tenants for the HYV paddy which works out to be higher than the rents for ordinary paddy grown during the *kharif* season. The average rent paid for the HYV turns out to be 4.79 quintals per acre where as for the ordinary paddy grown in the *kharif* season the average rent is approximately 3.18 quintals per acre. The gross productivity per acre is on an average 19.16 quintal for HYV, more than three times the average productivity of 6.36 quintals per acre for ordinary paddy. Landlords could afford to lease out at 25 per cent of the gross produce as rent since this actually works out to be more than the 50 per cent of share accruing to them while leasing out land for cultivation of ordinary paddy. It may be noted here that since the HYV paddy involves very high operational costs and the entire cost of inputs was borne by tenant the higher share of produce for the tenant may be considered necessary as an incentive to the tenant. Such a high share may well be a transitional stage. Their is a growing tendency for the leases to be of short duration with every new lease contract favouring the landlord. As we shall see in the context of irrigated areas, there is also an increasing tendency towards fixed cash rent

TABLE : 5.1 B

Unirrigated Area — Balarampur Village

*Sl. No. of Tenants**	*Tenant's Operational Holding (Acres)*	*Landlord's Ownership Holding (Acres)*	*Size of Leased Parcel (Acres)*	*Rents Per Acre (Quintals)*		*Rent as a Proportion of Gross Output (Per cent)*
				Under Share-Cropping	*Under Fixed Kind*	
1	*2*	*3*	*4*	*5*	*6*	*7*
11 a	2.48	9.00	1.50	2.50	-	50
b	-	10.00	0.50	3.00	-	25
12 a	7.00	8.00	1.00	2.00	-	50
b	-	7.00	0.30	5.00	-	25
13 a	5.53	12.00	1.00	1.71	-	50
b	-	10.00	1.28	3.90	-	25
14 a	8.00	9.00	1.00	1.80	-	50
b	-	9.00	1.00	4.25	-	25
15 a	7.94	6.00	1.00	4.00	-	50
b	-	2.00	1.00	4.00	-	50
c	-	-	0.60	5.00	-	25
16 a	5.00	15.00	2.50	3.36	-	50
b	-	8.00	0.60	3.75	-	25
17 a	5.50	2.00	1.00	3.00	-	50
b	-	2.00	1.00	3.00	-	50
c	-	-	1.00	5.00	-	25

Contd/-

TABLE : 5.1B (Contd.)

1	2	3	4	5	6	7
18 a	6.00	5.00	1.56	3.60	-	50
b	-	8.00	0.44	5.11	-	25
19	4.00	30.00	0.70	6.00	-	25
20 a	6.00	8.50	0.50	2.40	-	50
b	-	-	0.50	8.00	-	25
21 a	3.61	7.50	2.20	6.81	-	50
b	-	8.00	0.60	3.87	-	25
22	4.00	6.00	2.00	2.00	-	50
23	5.00	16.00	1.00	3.75	-	60
24	7.50	7.00	5.00	0.64	-	60
25	9.50	7.00	4.00	-	4.40	29
26	2.44	50.00	1.00	5.74	-	50

* If the tenant has more than one lease they have been recorded here separately, with alphabets following the serial number.

amenable to quick revisions and landlords trying to capitalise the gains of intensive cultivation of the HYV paddy.

The village Balarampur presents a complete shift in the tenurial arrangements in the 1990s. This transition is clearly visible when we compare our observations at both points of time— 1974-75 and 1990s. The village now enjoys controlled irrigation facilities all round the year with lift irrigation points from the river Chitrotpala. This has changed the agricultural scenario of the village. In 1974-75 there was only a single crop — generally paddy— grown in the village. But now because of assured irrigation facilities the village produces cash crops, largely vegetables of different varieties which has enabled better off farmers to improve their economic status, particularly those who have better access to resources have been successful in utilising the irrigation facility gainfully. But the condition of the poor tenant farmers or very small or marginal tenant farmers have become worse. For lack of resources these farmers have not been able to utilise the gain of irrigation, application of fertiliser or pesticide or improved variety of seeds. They have not been able to grow vegetables which requires all these inputs their economic status remained unchanged while that of the better off tenants have improved. It is worth noting here that some of the better off tenant farmers have been successful in obtaining favourable lease terms which hitherto was adverse to them. They are no more rendering free labour services nor do they give any 'gifts' to the lessors to keep them in good humour for continuance of the lease.[1] On the contrary some of the lessors prefer such tenants who have access to factor market or have resources of their own, because possession of factor inputs or access to factor market or one's own credit worthiness ensures use of better inputs and thereby increase the productivity which ultimately helps the lessors to obtain more output as his share/rent from the leased out plot. We have not given the figures in a separate table but in value terms rent accruing to the landlords in the 90s is more compared to that received in 1974-75.

Some of the lessors appear to prefer tenants who have sufficient labour power available in the family to be gainfully utilised in agricultural operations. These housholds, though, lack in resources, are preferred by lessors only because of the consideration that they can productively utilise the labour power available in the tenant family. Landlords in such cases provide improved seeds, fertiliser and bear the cost of irrigation but ultimately succeed in obtaining a larger share of the total produce which compensates more than the costs of the inputs provided to the tenants farmers. In most cases the landlords appropriate the costs of these inputs separately before the share or rent is collected from them. In cases, where the tenants are not in a position to buy inputs the landlords try to 'help'. They supply the inputs the cost of which is deducted at the time of harvest. After deducting the cost, the produce is shared by the landlord and the tenant, the former accruing a larger share of the total produce. In such cases the landlords also stipulate the crop to be produced by the tenant farmers because this enlarges the scope of gain. If cash crop is grown then the total value of their share accrued as rent will be comparatively more in terms of market prices. Lessors thus successfully capitalise the gains of increased productivity in agriculture.

Irrigated Areas : Region I : This region comprises village Lunahar in Cuttack district situated in the coastal region. The village has perennial canal water and cultivate HYV paddy as a second crop during the summer. In the *kharif* season, however, ordinary paddy is grown. The reasons as to why HYV paddy is not grown during the *kharif* season are first, canal irrigation is flow irrigation and therefore, the supply of water cannot be controlled and secondly, due to rains soil remains damp and therefore, is more prone to pest attacks. For both *kharif* and summer paddy cultivation, lease is generally given on cropsharing basis with 50 per cent of the gross output as rent for ordinary paddy and 25 per cent of the gross produce of HYV paddy as rent accruing to the landlord. The reason as to why landlords lease out on a 25/75 basis is same as stated in case of village Balarampur where tenants cultivate the HYV paddy during the summer. When the per acre productivity of HYV paddy can be almost three times more than ordinary paddy, more rent in actual terms may accrue to the landlord. In the year 1974-75 the summer crop of (HYV paddy) was affected because of pest attacks and other crop diseases and therefore, the output was adversely affected. As such we find (See Table 5.2A) that in many cases rents per acre measured in kind for HYV paddy works out to be lower than those under the ordinary paddy. Even then the average rent (i.e. 50 per cent of the gross produce) turns out to be 4.46 quintals per acre in case of ordinary paddy which is marginally higher than the rent per acre of HYV paddy i.e. 25 per cent of the gross produce which is 4.35 quintals of paddy. This indicates that in more favourable circumstances the rent per acre for HYV paddy will be comparatively higher than the rent paid for ordinary paddy.

Since, the leases are given entirely on sharecropping tenancy i.e. 50 per cent and 25 per cent of the gross produce accruing to the lessors for ordinary and HYV paddy respectively we cannot bring out the different ways the small tenants are being exploited so far as the cultivation of these crop is concerned. However, we will notice the different ways the lessors exploit the tenants.

The village Lunahar also shows significant changes. The perennial flow of canal water which was available all through the year during our visit in 1974-75, has been discontinued for a long period because of repair works. As a result, flow irrigation is not available and paddy of ordinary variety is grown during the *kharif* season followed by pulses or oil seeds growing as a subsidiary crop. This has effected a change the land tenure practices considerably.

TABLE : 5.2 A

Irrigated Region — I

*Sl. No. of Tenant**	*Tenant's Operational Holding (Acres)*	*Landlord's Ownership Holding (Acres)*	*Size of Leased Parcel (Acres)*	*Rent Per Acre (Quintals)*		*Rent as a proportion of Gross Output (Per cent)*	
				1975	*1990s*	*1975*	*1990s*
1	*2*	*3*	*4*	*5*	*6*	*7*	*8*
1 a	1.48	20.00	0.60	4.15	5.00	50	55
b	-	10.00	0.12	8.33	9.00	25	50
2 a	0.80	10.00	0.40	4.00	4.00	50	50
b	-	10.00	0.40	5.00	5.00	25	50
3 a	1.60	20.00	1.60	5.62	6.00	50	53
b	-	20.00	1.00	4.00	4.50	25	50
4 a	1.92	20.00	1.60	3.44	3.50	50	50
b	-	20.00	1.00	3.00	4.00	25	50
5 a	1.00	10.00	1.00	4.50	5.25	50	55
b	-	10.00	1.00	2.50	3.00	25	50
6 a	1.00	20.00	1.00	2.00	2.50	50	52
b	-	20.00	1.00	3.00	3.50	25	50
7	1.00	5.00	1.00	3.50	3.50	50	50
8 a	2.20	20.00	1.60	4.10	5.00	50	55
b	-	20.00	1.60	3.96	3.96	25	50
9	3.50	20.00	0.50	3.50	3.50	50	50

10 a	3.50	12.00	0.50	6.00	6.00	50	50
b	-	12.00	0.50	5.40	5.00	25	50
11 a	2.00	20.00	2.00	3.90	3.00	50	50
b	-	20.00	1.00	4.00	4.00	25	50
12 a	2.00	20.00	1.00	4.34	4.34	50	50
b	-	20.00	1.00	4.34	4.34	25	50
13	5.00	20.00	2.50	3.00	3.00	50	50

*** When the tenant has more than one lease unit, they have been recorded separately with alphabets attached to the serial number of the tenant.**

The *kharif* crop is now the major crop grown in the area. Earlier the lease was given on share-cropping basis but now it is being leased out on a fixed kind rent, because the landowners who lease out do not want to take the risk of losing the crop due to erratic monsoon rains. However, we also note that the big landlords when lease out to small tenant cultivators demand fixed kind rent while the better off tenant cultivators lease in under a crop sharing arrangement. This is largely because of the better resource status of the lessee. The small landowners who lease out under duress do not mind accepting any lease terms. They have hardly any alternative left to themselves.

For the second crop, pulses cultivated immediately after kharif season the sharing of crop is 50/50, because total harvest of these crops are not that significant. Big landlords do not insist on any change in the lease condition for this crop.

Region II : This region consists of the set of villages — Attabira, Parmanpur and Babebira — having canal irrigation all through the year. Irrigation facilities had been introduced in the area in the late 50s. But actual utilisation of this canal irrigation on a wide scale started only in the late 60s or early 70s when HYV was cultivated widely by the immigrant tenants. With the changes in the cropping pattern the tenurial system has changed entirely- the share-cropping system of land tenure has been replaced by fixed rent, which is paid mostly in cash. The system was fast replaced by fixed cash rents paid in advance. The only few cases where we noticed that the lease was given on fixed kind rent were the cases of small landowners, who needed paddy for their own consumption.

These are villages where we find some large tenants with large operational holdings (who have migrated from the neighbouring State — Andhra Pradesh) and that the lease parcels they lease in are generally not small. There are only a few cases where lease parcels are seen to be small and these are from lessors with very small holdings who cannot undertake self-cultivation for lack of labour and non-labour resources. (See Table 5.2 B).

TABLE : 5.2 B

Irrigated Region — II

*Sl. No. of the Tenant***	*Tenant's Operational Holding (Acres)*	*Landlord's Ownership Holding (Acres)*	*Size of Lease Parcel (Acres)*	*Rent Per Acre*			*Rent as Proportion of Gross Output (Per cent)*
				Under Fixed Kind (Qntls)	*Under Fixed Cash (Rs)*		
					1975	*1990*	
1	*2*	*3*	*4*	*5*	*6*	*7*	*8*
1	4.00	2.00	2.00	-	600	800	38.5
2 a	16.00	6.00	5.00	-	560	760	41.0*
b	-	7.00	5.00	-	500	700	41.0*
c	-	7.00	4.00	-	560	760	41.0*
d	-	2.00	2.00	-	480	680	41.0*
e***	-	-	2.00	-	100	100	41.0*
3 a	5.00	2.00	2.00	-	600	800	62.0*
b	-	25.00	3.00	-	600	800	62.0*
4 a	18.00	40.00	8.00	-	600	800	35.0*
b	-	9.00	4.00	-	600	800	35.0*
c	-	20.00	1.00	-	600	800	35.0*
d	-	3.00	3.00	-	600	800	35.0*
e	-	8.00	1.00	-	600	800	35.0*
5	2.50	23.00	2.50	-	600	800	46.0
6	4.00	4.00	4.00	-	600	800	60.0

Contd/-.

TABLE: 5.2b (Contd.)

1	*2*	*3*	*4*	*5*	*6*	*7*	*8*
7 a	16.00	14.00	10.00	-	600	800	31.0*
b	-	15.00	3.00	-	600	800	31.0*
c	-	3.00	3.00	-	600	800	31.0*
8 a	7.20	40.00	3.50	-	600	800	30.0*
b	-	-	1.50	-	600	800	30.0*
9	5.80	1.00	0.80	7.50	-	-	67.0
10 a	5.00	30.00	3.00	-	700	900	48.0
b	-	1.00	1.00	7.50	-	-	33.0*
c	-	1.00	1.00	7.50	-	-	33.0*
11	2.00	2.00	2.00	7.50	-	-	31.0
12	4.00	20.00	3.00	-	720	1000	30.0
13	2.00	15.00	2.00	-	720	1000	33.0
14 a	5.50	25.00	3.00	-	720	1000	46.0
b	-	-	1.00	-	600	800	46.0
15 a	3.00	15.00	0.80	-	625	850	36.0*
b	-	18.00	1.00	-	600	800	36.0*
16	2.50	4.00	2.00	7.50	-	-	33.0
17 a	2.00	1.80	1.80	7.50	-	-	30.0*
b	-	17.00	0.20	7.50	-	-	30.0*
18 a	7.00	25.00	2.00	-	720	1000	41.0*
b	-	15.00	3.00	-	600	800	41.0*
c	-	9.00	1.00	-	600	800	41.0*

d	-	20.00	1.00	-	600	800	41.0*
19 a	12.00	17.00	4.00	-	600	800	46.0*
b	-	2.00	1.00	-	600	800	46.0*
20	20.00	40.00	20.00	-	400	600	31.0*

Note * The tenant with multiple leases reported an average figure for total rent paid by him as a proportion of total gross produce on all the leased units.

** When a tenant has more than one lease, the lease units are recorded separately with aplhabets following the serial number of the tenant.

*** This plot was leased out by 'Railways'.

In is Table 5.2 B we notice that the per acre fixed cash rent varies from Rs 400/- to Rs 720/-. The only exceptional case where the rent is only Rs. 100/- per acre has been a lease from the Railways. But in most cases the rent is Rs 600/-. Out of 34 cases where fixed rent is being paid in as much as in 22 cases Rs 600/- is paid as rent per acre. There are five cases where the per acre rent is Rs 700/- or more. Table 5.2 C gives the frequency distribution of leases taken on fixed cash or kind rent.

TABLE : 5.2 C

Frequency Distribution of Leased by Rent

Rent Per Acre (Rupees)		*Number of Leased Units Paying Rent*	
1975	1990	1975	1990
100		1*	-
400	600	1	1
480	680	1	1
500	700	1	-
560	760	2	2
600	800	29**	23
625	850	1	1
700	900	1	1
720	1000	4	4

Notes * Leased out by Railways.

** Includes 7 leases on fixed kind rent whose money equivalent was Rs 600/- per acre.

It will, however, be noted from Table 5.2 B that the few cases, where rent exceeds Rs 600/- per acre, are the cases when large landowners have leased out to relatively smaller tenants, who are economically not better off (See Tenants Serial Nos. 10a, 12, 13, 14a, 15a, and 18a). It is further interesting to note that in cases when they lease in from small landowners, the tenants usually pay less as rent whereas when they lease in from large landlords the same tenants are asked to pay higher rents. In other words the tenants who pay less than Rs 600/- as rent per acre are mostly economically better off than those who pay more, in relation to their respective landlords (See Serial Nos. 2a, b, c and d, and 20).

Considering rent as a proportion of gross output (See Column 7 of Table 5.2 B) it may be observed that rent constitutes less than 50 per cent of the aggregate produce barring only three cases (Serial Nos. 3, 6 and 9 with operational holding between 4-6 acres). The average figures of rent as a proportion of gross output are given in Table 5.2 D. Tenants with operational holdings below 5 acres pay comparatively a higher rent than those with operational holdings between 5-10 acres. Those with operational holdings of above 10 acres pay Rs 611/- as rent per acre while tenants operating with less than 5 acres pay Rs 642/- as rent per acre. Similarly when we observe rent as a proportion of aggregate output we note that tenants with less than 5 acres of operational holdings pay 42 per cent of the gross output whereas those with above 10 acres operational holdings pay only 36 per cent. Thus we can say that small tenants (with less than 5 acres of operational holdings) are more vulnerable to exploitation than big tenants (with more than 10 acres of operational holdings).

Significant changes appear to have taken place in the Irrigated Region II comprising Attabira, Parmanpur and Babebira. During the first survey there was greater bias in favour of immigrant tenants from Andhra Pradesh. As stated earlier there was a large number of tenants who had migrated from the neighbouring state of Andhra Pradesh, these cultivators are industrious, more resourceful and are able to lease in land parcel at a competitive rent. They appear to be more effective as lessees compared to the native tenant cultivators. The same situation still prevails even now in 1990s. The Andhra tenant cultivators not only become effective as lessees but also obtain land parcels which are close to the canal, close to their residences and therefore, have all advantages. Being in proximity these tenant cultivators can afford to put in more labour power and better supervision on the field and thereby could reap a better harvest. Therefore, they could

TABLE : 5.2 D

Rent as Proportion of Output and Gross Productivity Per Acre According to Size — Groups

Size of Operational Holding of Tenant (Acres)	Number of Leases	Rent Per Acres (Rs)	Rent as Proportion of Output (Per cent)	Gross Productivity Per Acre (Rs)
5 Acres and Below	15	642	42	1528
5-10 Acres	10	636	43	1479
Above 10 Acres	16	611	36	1572

afford to pay a higher rent They do not have the risks of water scarcity or time consumption in reaching the plots etc. In fact some of the Andhra tenants have leased in land parcels just across the canal and close to their residential plots from where they can supervise easily the different agricultural operations.

Some of the landlords have started feeling that they should lease out land parcels to the native tenant cultivators rather than leasing out to the Andhra tenants. This is a new trend. Such preference arises because the landowners feel that their land units will not be spoiled because of application of fertilisers in large quantities. But what is more important is that the lessors feel that they could appropriate other benefits (like free labour services, etc.) from the native tenant cultivators which was hitherto not possible to appropriate from Andhra tenant cultivators. The Andhra tenants did not have any other obligations except the few bags of paddy or cash advance which they have to pay as rent. The lessor did not mind to rent out the land even for a lesser quantity of rent because the benefits (other than the rent) like free unpaid labour services etc. could compensate the higher amount of rent which the Andhra tenant would have been prepared to pay. This is a major consideration for which they prefer the native tenant cultivators. But such cases are very rare. The tenant cultivators belonging to the locality feel obliged and do not hesitate to render free labour services or giving free gifts during the festive occasions in the form of vegetables, free bullock labour, the bullock-carts to go to neighbouring places etc.

The lease duration is usually very short either for a single crop or for both crops—*kharif* and summer crops. When enquired about the purpose of giving short period lease the reason given was that the contract may be enhanced in the next lease, i.e. the rent for the land if possible could be raised by changing the tenant cultivators. During the 90s almost all leases were short term leases. In almost all cases the cash rent paid in advance has been increased.

Another important change that has been noticed during our second survey in the 1990s is the transition in the cropping pattern. There are more than two crops which could be harvested now, and these are mostly cash crops apart from the HYV paddy which is harvested from the field during summer. Groundnuts or vegetables which hitherto were not cultivated, are being cultivated by some of the tenant cultivators. In such cases rents have gone up very high largely because of the increased productivity of land.

During the second survey, it has also been observed that in a few cases (not in our sample villages but in the neighbourhood), *ber* a kind of fruit which bears only once a year is being cultivated in a scientific manner, which yields high returns from land. It is expected (as some of the landlords are of the opinion) that cultivation of this crop will gain further momentum.

The situation of the very small or marginal landholders is still precarious. They still face the problem of undertaking self-cultivation largely because the cost of factor inputs are so high which they could hardly afford. Under such circumstances, they have no other alternative but to lease out land under duress. Situation and status of these small and marginal landholders have not changed over the decade. Similarly pure tenant farmers with small operational holdings have been adversely affected during 90s. It appears they perhaps could withstand the competition in the lease market. The increase in cash rent with every new lease perhaps is the major reason. These poor tenants could not afford to pay the enhanced rents. Neither they have their own resources nor do they have an easy access to the factor market for lack of creditworthiness. Some of these tenants in our sample have withdrawn themselves from the lease market. They have started looking for other occupation: like tailoring etc.

Another development is the wide use of tractors in carrying out various agricultural operation. In 1974-75 there were a couple of tractors while in the 1990s there are multiple number of tractors used in the production process. This helps in removing the problem of labour, reducing the cost and timely completing the various agricultural operations.

Cash Crop Area: The village Nalabanta produces sugarcane as the principal crop. Other crops like paddy, mung etc. are also being cultivated in the area. There exist different systems of land tenure arrangements for the different crops grown in the area. While for sugarcane the rents are paid in fixed cash, paddy is cultivated under all the three systems — share-cropping, fixed kind or fixed cash rent. For the other minor crops like mung the produce is being shared between the tenant and the landlord. But this we will discuss later in this chapter. In the case of paddy cultivated under a cropsharing system the aggregate output is usually shared on a 60/40 basis the larger share being appropriated by landlords, but in the case of minor crops the share varied widely. In cases where paddy is cultivated on fixed kind rent the rent varied between 5.50 quintals to 8.0 quintals, the more recent lessees paying a higher rent.

Since, a particular tenant might lease in land parcels under varying systems of rent payment and as some of the tenants grow exclusively paddy or sugarcane we have given here (See Table - 5.3 A) the frequency distribution of all leases by tenancy types and by crops. We have indicated that land parcels are leased out under various modes of rent payment particularly when paddy is grown. In order to compare the rent payments under the different systems we have converted actual rents paid under share-cropping and fixed kind rent into their money equivalents at Rs 80/- per quintal which was the prevailing price in the village in the year 1974-75 after the harvest. (See Table 5.3 B). From the table we could observe that many of the tenants have small operational holdings. There are only a few who operate with holdings of more than 5 acres. Only in a few cases we notice that rent is being paid in fixed cash, and therefore, it will not be proper to make any general conclusion on the fixed cash system of tenancy. However, in two out of the three cases, we observe that fixed rents paid by tenants with weak economic status are higher and in these two cases the lessors are big landowners.

TABLE : 5.3 A

Number of Leases According to Tenurial Types Village — Nalabanta

	Under Share-Cropping	*Fixed Kind Rent*	*Fixed Cash Rent*	*Total*
Growing Paddy	11	25	3	39
Growing Sugarcane	-	-	25	25

We also note a similar situation in case of tenants leasing in under a fixed kind system of rent payment. Here, too we observe that small lessees with operational holdings of less than three acres do pay a higher amount of rent. In many cases these are tenants who lease in from landlords with better economic status. Similarly under cropsharing tenancy small tenants are seen to be paying more rents compared to those with larger operational holdings. We note that per acre rent under both sharecropping and fixed kind system turns out to be higher for small tenants operating with holdings below 5 acres compared to tenants with operational holdings of more than five acres. Rent under fixed kind and cash systems constitutes a smaller proportion of the gross output in case of small tenants whereas in case of bigger tenants the proportion of rent to gross output is higher (See Table 5.3 C). On an average we find that fixed cash rents per acre are higher than the money equivalent of rents per acre under share-cropping or fixed kind systems. When we compare the rents as a proportion of the aggregate output we observe that the maximum proportion is being paid under the share-cropping tenancy, whereas in case of fixed kind system it is less and it is the lowest in the case of fixed cash system. In order to bring out the differences in the

TABLE : 5.3 B

Cash Crop Area — Village : Nalabanta

Sl. No. of the Tenant*		Tenant's Total Operational Holding (Acres)	Landlord's Ownership Holding (Acres)	Size of Leased Parcel (Acres)	Actual Rent Paid: Under Share-Cropping (Quintals)	Actual Rent Paid: Paddy Under Fixed Kind (Quintals)* or Cash (Rs)**	Actual Rent Paid: Sugarcane Fixed Cash (Rs)	Cash Rent for Money Equivalent of Rent Per Acre: Paddy (Rs)	Cash Rent for Money Equivalent of Rent Per Acre: Sugarcane (Rs)	Rent as Proportion of Output: Paddy (Per cent)	Rent as Proportion of Output: Sugarcane (Per cent)
1		2	3	4	5	6	7	8	9	10	11
1		2.20	15.00	1.60	-	12.80*	-	640	-	40	-
2		0.40	20.00	0.40	-	300**	-	750	-	20	-
3	a	7.30	10.00	3.20	24.80*	-	-	620	-	60	-
4	b	-	10.00	2.40	-	-	1500	-	625	-	39
	c	-	5.00	0.60	-	-	375	-	625	-	38
	d	-	7.00	0.20	-	-	150	-	750	-	39
	e	-	3.00	0.20	-	150**	-	750	-	43	-
4		3.50	10.00	2.50	24.00	-	1875	768	750	60	51
5	a	2.50	7.00	1.40	-	9.80*	10.50	560	750	43	47
	b	-	4.00	0.60	-	4.20*	450	560	750	43	48
6	a	3.20	5.00	0.20	-	-	140	-	700	-	31
	b	-	4.00	0.60	-	-	390	-	650	-	31

Contd./-

Table: 5.3b (Contd.)

1		2	3	4	5	6	7	8	9	10	11
7		5.20	4.60	3.60	18.00	-	2760	400	600	60	48
8	a	3.00	8.00	1.20	8.00	-	-	530	-	60	-
	b	-	12.00	0.90	6.00	-	-	530	-	60	-
	c	-	6.00	0.30	2.00	-	-	530	-	60	-
	d	-	8.00	0.80	-	4.80*	-	480	-	-	34
9	a	5.60	6.00	0.60	-	3.00*	-	400	-	40	-
	b	-	8.00	1.40	-	7.00*	-	400	-	40	-
10		1.50	10.00	1.20	-	864**	-	720	-	-	45
11	a	6.00	5.00	1.00	-	6.00*	-	480	-	40	-
	b	-	10.00	1.00	-	6.00*	-	480	-	40	-
12	a	4.60	8.00	0.60	4.60	-	-	625	-	60	-
	b	-	7.00	0.75	5.80	-	-	620	-	60	-
	c	-	7.00	3.25	25.60	-	-	620	-	60	-
13	a	4.00	6.00	2.40	-	12.96*	-	432	-	42	-
	b	-	10.00	0.50	-	-	300	-	600	-	25
	c	-	10.00	0.50	-	-	300	-	600	-	25
14	a	2.50	5.00	0.40	-	2.80*	-	560	-	44	-
	b	-	5.00	0.60	-	4.20*	-	560	-	44	-
15		2.50	6.00	2.00	-	11.00*	1200	440	600	45	44
16		1.80	8.00	1.80	-	11.70*	936	520	520	30	40
17		1.55	9.50	1.55	-	11.25*	900	600	600	45	38
18		1.45	9.50	1.45	-	10.80*	942	600	650	61	37

19		8.00	8.00	8.00	40.50	-	1050	810	750	60	70
20	a	2.80	8.00	1.20	13.50	-	-	600	-	60	-
	b	-	7.00	1.20	13.50	-	-	600	-	60	-
21	a	2.70	7.00	1.20	-	-	720	320	600	35	47
	b	-	7.00	1.00	-	4.00	600	320	600	35	47
22	a	3.40	5.00	1.00	5.40	-	1000	428	1000	60	70
	b	-	8.00	0.20	1.20	-	200	500	1000	60	70
	c	-	8.00	1.60	8.40	-	1600	520	1000	60	70
23		2.60	13.00	2.00	-	15.00*	1500	600	750	43	60
24		2.00	15.00	2.00	-	14.00*	1200	560	600	58	47
25	a	2.00	9.50	1.50	-	11.25*	900	600	600	60	46
	b	-	4.00	0.50	-	3.75*	300	600	600	45	46

* When the tenant has more than one lease, the lease units are recorded separately, with alphabets following the serial number of the tenant.

TABLE : 5.3 C

Rent Per Acre, Rent as Share of Gross Produce and Gross Product Per Acre According to Size - Groups of Tenants — Village Nalabanta

Size of Tenant's Operational Holding	*Money Equivalent of Rent Per Acre*			*Rent as Share of Gross Produce*			*Gross Productivity Per Acre*		
	Under Share-Cropping (Rs)	*Under Fixed Kind (Rs)*	*Under Cash Rent (Rs)*	*Under Share-Cropping Per cent*	*Under Fixed Kind Per cent*	*Under Cash Rent Per cent*	*Under Share Cropping (Rs)*	*Under Fixed Kind (Rs)*	*Under Cash Rent (Rs)*
Below 5 Acres	685	527	750	60	41	30	1142	1317	2500
5-10 Acres	536	425	750	60	42	43	893	1187	1769

proportion of rent paid by the tenants we have classified all tenants into two categories — small, with operational holdings of less than 5 acres, large, with operational holdings of more than 5 acres. It may be observed that while small tenants pay higher rents under cropsharing and fixed kind systems, both categories of tenants pay equal amount of rent under fixed cash systems. But when the actual rent paid per acre is converted into the proportion of the total output the small tenants appear to pay less. This is largely because the gross productivity per acre works out to be more in case of small tenants. Another noticeable feature here is that gross productivity per acre turns out to be higher (it is in fact the maximum) in case of fixed rent than under share-cropping for both class of tenants big as well as the small.

Sugarcane is the main cash crop grown in this village Nalabanta. For the cultivation of this crop land parcels are leased out entirely on fixed cash system. The rent per acre vary between Rs 520/- to Rs 1,000/- per acre, the highest amount of rents being paid by a petty tenant.[2] Increase in the per acre rent is a recent phenomenon. The frequency distribution of lease units according to the amount of rent paid is given in Table 5.3D. In order to bring out the differences in the amount of rent paid per acre and the gross productivity per acre we have classified the tenants into two categories — small, with below 5 acres of operational holdings and large, with more than 5 acres of operational holding, and we notice that tenants below 5 acres pay a higher rent compared to those who have more than 5 acres of land (operational holding). But what is significant is that per acre gross productivity is more in case of small tenants. As a result of this the actual rent paid by small tenants turns out to be less (as a proportion of gross produce paid as rent) than bigger tenants. (See Table 5.3E).

In the village Nalabanta producing cash crop mainly sugarcane or vegetables, situations have further deteriorated from the tenants' point of view. Appropriation of exorbitant rent coupled with extraction of free or underpaid labour services still continue to prevail.

TABLE : 5.3 D

Frequency Distribution of Leases According to Rent Per Acre Village—Nalabanta

Rent Per Acre (Rs)	*Number of Leases*
520	1
600	10
625	2
650	2
700	1
750	6
1000	3

TABLE : 5.3 E

Rent Per Acre, Rent as Share of Gross Output and Gross Productivity Per Acre According to Size - Groups of Tenants

Size of Tenant's Operational Holding	*Rent per Acre (Rs)*	*Rent as Share of Gross Produce (Per cent)*	*Gross Productivity Per Acre (Rs)*
Below 5 Acres	694	46.4	1509
5 to 10 Acres	670	47.0	1476

For example, land is lease out now not on cropsharing basis but on fixed rent basis. The amount of this fixed rent is gradually increasing particularly when it is rented out for cultivation of cash crop. For sugarcane cultivation the minimum rent asked for by landowners is Rs 2,600/- while for other cash crop it is Rs 2000/-. Tenant cultivators have to agree to such lease terms because they do not have any other alternative. The infrastructure they have with them (plough share, bullocks, bullock-cart etc.) cannot be wound up.

Similarly, for paddy the rents have also gone up. In case of share-cropping the arrangement was sharing the output on 50/50 basis in 1973-74 while it has been 60/40 now in the1990s, 40 per cent being shared by tenant. This includes the cost of cultivation i.e. the cost of all factor inputs inclusive of the labour power involved in the production process that is borne by the tenant.

In some cases, fixed rent also is demanded by the landlords which works out to be sharing the harvest equally. But in this case the tenant has the risk — the risk of losing the crop due to weather uncertainties or natural calamity. The landlords, except in rare cases, are rigid on appropriating the fixed rent, agreed between him and the tenant.

Whether it is share-cropping or fixed rent arrangement, the tenant farmers have to render unpaid or underpaid labour services to the landlord, give free gifts in order to keep the landlords in good humour so that the lease is continued. Most the landlords expect such services from the lessees. Land available for cultivation being limited, puts the landlords in an advantageous position. Alternative employment opportunity being limited the tenant farmers have no other alternative but to agree to lease terms and conditions even if it is adverse. As such rents have been increasing in every 2 to 3 years period, whether it is cash rent, fixed kind rent or share-cropping system. The landlords appropriate higher rents from the lessees. As stated earlier for sugarcane cultivation the rent has gone up as high as Rs 2,600/- under share-cropping arrangement it is 60/40 (or in some cases it is 65/35) the higher share accruing to the landowners, and if it is fixed rent it is 8 quintals of paddy per acre. Even under share-cropping arrangement the lessees are afraid of losing the lease if the harvest is not of sizeable amount. In other words the output being small the share of the landowner will be smaller. The tenants in such cases are evicted, the lease is not renewed but is given to some other tenant.

It is often noted, that better quality of land is leased out under crop-sharing arrangement. The quality of land being better the output is expected to be higher. Therefore, if such land is given under share-cropping system, the lessors will gain. This comparative gain induces the landowners to lease out land under cropsharing basis.

In case of inferior land, where output is expected to be small or the productivity is low the land parcels are usually leased out on fixed rent basis. If land parcels are prone to drought or flood or other natural calamities, the yield is expected to be low and therefore, the landlords' share is going to be small. The landlords therefore prefer to lease out such pieces of land on fixed rent.

In either case, we note that the landlords do not take the chance of losing the rent of the leased out land parcels. Depending on circumstances, the quality of land and the infrastructure like irrigation etc. the lease terms are dictated by the landowners and the tenants, under duress, have to lease in, even if the lease terms are adverse to them.

Tribal Areas : We have selected villages, predominantly inhabited by tribals, from two different districts of the state. Of the four, three villages — Gumagarh, G. Udayagiri and Raikia are from Phulbani District and the remaining village Mendhakhia is from Udala sub-division of Mayurbhanj district. In the first set of villages we notice the leases are given entirely on share-cropping basis where as in Medhakhia multiple system of land tenure practices exist — where some tenants cultivate under share-cropping basis, some cultivate under fixed cash rent and only one cultivates under fixed kind rent. In all these, paddy is the major and very often the only crop grown. There are minor irrigation projects in all these villages except the village Raikia. But these projects do not have sufficient water potential for a second crop to be cultivated. In majority cases, no second crop is grown except a few cases where tamarind is cultivated by the tribals. However, these are grown generally on the homestead land of the tribals, as such no question of rent on this arises.

In the three villages of Phulbani district land parcels are leased out entirely on a sharecropping basis. The share of paddy accruing to the landlord as rent is 50 per cent of the gross produce in all cases (See Table 5.4A). Thus the differences in actual rents paid per acre (See Column 6 of the Table) reflect the differences in productivity of different plots. Generally speaking yield per acre is seen to be higher on smaller lease parcels (See Column 4 of the Table), especially when the tenants' operational holding shown in column 2, happens to be small, too. One possible reason may be that better lands are parcelled out and leased out in small proportions to tenants and tenants try to maximise the productivity in order to eke out a living from these small parcels. This seems to be more reasonable when we note that these petty tenants have very small operational holding of which a major proportion is the leased in land. Alternative sources of earning being scarce and uncertain tenants try to put in more of inputs, family labour input in particular, in these small parcels of land, so that it may provide some subsistence to these marginal tenants. This argument is further corrorborated by the statements given by the landlords (lessors) that land parcels when leased out to small tenants in small sizes, the lessees work harder and thus they are able to maximise the amount of rent appropriated by them.

Conditions of lease are however, different in Mendhakhia. Here we notice the land parcels are being leased out both under cropsharing or fixed cash systems. There is only a solitary case where fixed kind rent is paid by the tenant (See Tenant Serial No. 22b, in Table 5.4B). One noticeable feature of the land lease market here in this village is, that most of the lessors are very small landholders and except two (Sl. Nos. 25 a and 34) where the landowners possess more than 30 acres, all the rest who have

TABLE : 5.4A

Tribal Area — Gumagarh, G. Udaygiri and Raikia

Sl No. of Tenant	*Tenants's Operational Holding (Acres)*	*Landlord's Owned Holding (Acres)*	*Size of Leased Parcel (Quintals)*	*Actual Rent Paid in Kind Kind (Quintals)*	*Rent per acre in Kind (Quintals)*
Village: Gumagarh					
1.	0.40	20.00	0.40	1.50	3.75
2.	0.80	20.00	0.40	1.50	3.75
3.	3.30	2.00	2.00	6.00	3.00
4.	1.60	30.00	0.60	2.50	4.37
5.	0.65	2.00	0.25	1.00	4.00
6.	0.80	30.00	0.80	2.40	3.00
Village: G. Udaygiri					
7.	2.00	3.80	2.00	6.00	3.00
8.	5.00	3.00	3.00	6.00	2.00
9.	1.85	40.00	1.00	3.00	3.00
10.	6.00	3.80	1.00	2.00	2.00
11.	8.00	40.00	1.00	3.00	3.00
12.	1.80	20.00	0.60	2.50	4.37
13.	1.80	2.50	0.25	0.50	2.00
14.	9.00	40.00	4.00	8.00	2.00
Village: Raikia					
15.	1.00	17.00	1.00	4.00	4.00
16.	4.00	17.00	4.00	12.00	3.00
17.	1.80	3.00	1.00	5.00	5.00
18.	12.00	17.00	12.00	30.00	2.50
19.	1.40	17.00	0.60	4.00	6.70

leased out on fixed cash system are the small 'landlords'. Many of these small landowners do not have sufficient economic support to go in for self-cultivation and therefore, they lease out seeking employment elsewhere.

In order to compare the differences in the rents paid under the various lease systems, we have converted the rents paid both under share-cropping and under fixed kind rent into money equivalents (See Columns 8 and 9 in Table 5.4B). For the purpose of conversion of money equivalent of the actual rent paid we have taken the prevailing price of Rs 100/- per quintal of paddy in the village. It may be observed that the money equivalent of rent per acre under fixed cash system is generally lower than that paid under the crop-sharing system. The average money equivalent of rent per acre is Rs 235/- in case of cropsharing tenancy whereas it is Rs 201/- in case of fixed cash rent system. This , however, goes against the usual expectations (and the more general experience under conditions of rising prices of agricultural commodities) that fixed cash rents are generally higher than the rents under share system. It may be due to the fact that most of the landlords who have preferred fixed cash rents in the present case are economically weaker and therefore, prefer cash rents which is generally collected prior to harvest. A possible reason may be that these lessors try to avoid fluctuations in rent which they will appropriate under sharecropping.

We arrive at a similar conclusion when we compare the proportion of gross produce paid out as rent under various lease systems. Under the sharecropping tenancy we have lessors who appropriate 50 per cent of the aggregate output where as in case of fixed cash rent (except tenants serial No. 28a) the proportion of gross produce accruing to the landlord as rent works out to be less than 50 per cent (on an average 32 per cent). But the productivity per acre turns out to be higher in the fixed rent system. In fact the actual figures of gross productivity per acre are

TABLE : 5.4 B

Tribal Area — Village Mendhakhia

*Sl. No. of Tenant**	*Tenant's Operational Holding (Acres)*	*Landlord's Ownership Holding (Acres)*	*Size of Leased Parcel (Acres)*	*Actual Rents Paid* Under Share-Cropping (Qntls)	Under Fixed Kind (Qntls)	Under Fixed Cash (Rs)	*Rent in Rs Per Acre* Money Equivalent of Share	Money Equivalent of Fixed Kind	In Fixed Cash	*Rent as Proportion of Gross Output (Per cent)*
1	2	3	4	5	6	7	8	9	10	11
20	4.00	4.00	2.00	4.50	-	-	225	-	-	50
21	4.50	4.00	2.00	6.00	-	-	300	-	-	50
22 a	4.50	2.00	1.00	2.00	-	-	200	-	-	50
b		30.00	1.50	-	3.75	-	-	250	-	41
23	2.50	30.00	1.00	2.50	-	-	250	-	-	50
24	4.50	30.00	2.00	4.80	-	-	240	-	-	50
25 a	7.50	30.00	4.00	-	-	800	-	-	200	38
b		2.00	0.50	1.00	-	-	200	-	-	50
26	6.50	30.00	2.50	5.62	-	-	225	-	-	50
27 a	8.00	4.00	2.00	4.00	-	-	200	-	-	50
b		2.50	1.50	-	-	300	-	-	200	27
28 a	0.88	0.18	0.18	-	-	60	-	-	330	60
b	-	1.50	0.35	1.00	-	-	286	-	-	50

29	3.50	5.00	2.50	-	-	500	-	-	200	25
30	2.00	2.00	1.00	-	-	180	-	-	180	43
31	1.00	2.00	0.50	-	-	50	-	-	100	33
32	6.50	4.00	1.50	-	-	300	-	-	200	20
33	3.00	1.00	1.00	-	-	200	-	-	200	16
34	5.50	30.00	1.50	-	-	300	-	-	200	23
35	1.00	3.00	1.00	2.25	-	-	225	-	-	50

* The tenant holds more than one lease, shown separately here, with alphabets following the serial number.

Rs. 470/- under the share-cropping system and Rs 705/- under fixed rent system of land tenure. This suggests that productivity of land is higher under fixed rent system than under share-cropping. It may due to the fact that the tenant by certain knows anything he gross more than the rent paid to the landlord will accrue to him. Therefore, the tenant puts in his maximum effort to increase the productivity of land.

In tribal areas situations during the 90s have not changed. The tenants in many cases are still rackrented and have to lease in under onerous lease conditions. Besides the rent the tenant cultivators are subjected to render free labour services or else they involve the risk of losing the lease. In tribal areas the alternative employment opportunities being almost absent, the tenants have to seek lease parcels even under the most adverse lease terms.

We briefly summarise here some of the common observations noticed in the lease conditions in different areas that we have discussed above.

(i) We have seen that the major factor influencing the terms and conditions of the lease is the relative economic status of lessor and lessee. Whether it is fixed kind rent or cash rent or share-cropping system of tenancy, the relative socio-economic positions of landlords and tenants, generally seem to play a vital role in determining the conditions of lease. As we have observed it is the smaller tenants who pay a higher rent than bigger ones. The smaller tenants have leased in mostly from big landlords, rather it would be more proper to say that big landowners are more interested in leasing out to small tenants (tenants here include pure tenants and small owner-tenants with medium size operational holdings i.e. between 3-8 acre size class). Contrary to this big tenants and owner-tenants operating in medium size classes are seen to be leasing in mostly from small and big landlords as well. But when small owner-tenants and pure tenants are comparatively weaker in relation to their landlords, the landlords are seen to be extracting more rent from these tenants, whereas in case of big tenants, the rent paid is lower. Therefore, we may say that the relative socio-economic status of lessor and lessee largely influences the lease conditions. This situation is clearly seen when a particular tenant is seen to be leasing in from different lessors with different resource positions, and paying different amount of rent to different landlords. The situation still prevails during the 90s. The small tenants or tenants with weak economic status bear the burden of the adverse lease conditions.

(ii) We also observe that gross productivity per acre is generally higher for land leased in under fixed rent (both kind and cash) than under sharecropping. This might be largely due to the fact that under share tenancy the tenant contributes generally half of the gross produce as rent while the landlord does not share any cost of production. Therefore, the tenant probably shirks from investing in land because returns to each additional unit of capital, labour and fertiliser and other factor inputs invested in land, will not accrue to him in total. Under fixed rent system the tenant is at least sure that additional units of capital and other inputs invested in the leased in land will yield him more of output. The total benefit accruing to the tenant will be more after the fixed amount of rent is paid to the lessor.

(iii) Gross productivity per acre turns out to be higher in case of small tenants. This is found in all the sample villages. In a situation where alternative sources of employment are quite uncertain, small tenants try to get maximum output of leased in land in order to raise subsistence. However, in irrigated regions, with assured and perennial irrigation facilities gross productivity is seen to be higher in case of large tenant cultivators. This is because the bigger tenants have more resources at their disposal which could be invested in agriculture.

(iv) The fixed cash rent system prevails in two widely different sets of economic circumstances — first, where economically depressed 'landlords' lease out under financial difficulties generally of fixed cash rents. In this case fixed cash rent per acre turns out to be lower than the money equivalent of fixed kind rent or of the actual share rent. We have also observed a second category of landlords almost similar to this above type of lessors, who lease out land under fixed cash system. These landowners are also economically weaker section and therefore, are in great need of money. They borrow certain amount of money from the tenant and in turn 'lease out' to him a parcel of land to be cultivated for a specific period and to raise a fixed number of crops, depending upon the amount of credit that he has availed of from the lessee. In this category of lessors also, we find the rent to be low. Unlike the first two categories of lessors there are landlords who are economically well up, who also adopt this method of leasing out since this is a more convenient method of appropriating rent under the guise of mortgage of land for a 'loan' from the tenant. It is, however, a form of concealed tenancy. Since this is an easy trick to escape from the impact of land reform legislation restricting tenancy, landlords are seen to resort to this method widely in some of the areas of the state.

In the Irrigated Region II, we observe that cropsharing and fixed kind rent system of tenancy have been gradually displaced by fixed cash rent system. Here big tenants, some of whom are migrants from Andhra State advanced cash rents generally at the time when the contract is made. While the big tenants have acquired leases for longer duration for 3 to 4 years generally, the lease periods have been conspicuously shortened for small tenants and the threat of eviction has increased for them. The cash rents also get revised continually after every short lease. In this Irrigated Region II fixed cash rent exceed money equivalent of rent paid under fixed kind or under share-cropping system.

SECTION II

Sharing of Subsidary Crops and By-Products

So far we have discussed about the terms and conditions in relation to the principal crop produced i.e. paddy (including the HYV) and sugarcane (in the cash crop area alone), where we have noted the influence of the relative resource position of the tenant and the landlord on the lease conditions. We have observed that tenants with weak socio-economic position are more vulnerable to exploitation by landowners with better economic status, whereas tenants with better economic resources are less vulnerable to such exploitation. We have noticed that while the small tenants are asked to pay more rent, the big tenants generally pay a comparatively low rent. A further probe particularly in relation to subsidiary or minor crops raised, and sharing of by-products and other terms and conditions like unpaid labour services rendered by the tenants, 'free gifts' either offered or attached with the lease etc. will reveal more interesting features of the terms and conditions of lease.

Sharing Arrangements of Subsidiary Crops

Of the four different areas considered here, the second crop is not grown in unirrigated areas, except in a few cases. This is largely because the land dries up soon after the harvest of the principal crop. This is particularly the case with village Bhalliamunda in Bolangir district. But in the village Balarampur, the tenant cultivators are mostly engaged in cultivating the HYV paddy in a village across the river. But unlike these two villages we find in

Nalabanta, (the village mainly growing cash crop) the tenants also raise a second crop either mung, or paddy or *channa*. So far as the irrigated villages are concerned, in Attabira tenants grow the HYV paddy in the summer as a second crop, in Lunahar in many cases the tenants are engaged in growing HYV paddy. We have already discussed the cropsharing arrangements of the HYV paddy grown as a second crop in the villages Lunahar and Attabira. In Lunahar there is a solitary case where *channa* is grown and in this case the landlord appropriates 90 per cent of the gross produce as rent leaving only 10 per cent for the tenant. The particular landlord concerned reported that since the tenant does not have to toil much and spend little for the cultivation of this crop, the proportion of produce accruing to the tenant should be less.

So far as the village Nalabanta is concerned, mung is largely cultivated as a second crop. In some cases we also find paddy is grown as a second crop. About sharing of paddy we have commented earlier in this chapter, and we have noted that while in some cases it is shared on a 60/40 basis, in some cases it is 50 per cent for both or is cultivated under a fixed rent system. But in the case of mung which is a second crop we find many instances where it is shared equally between the lessors and lessees. In two cases 25 per cent and in another two cases 60 per cent and in one case 65 per cent of the total mung produce was appropriated by the respective landlords.

But in the unirrigated areas particularly in the village Bhalliamunda, there were only two cases where mung is grown and the gross produce was shared equally between landlord and tenant. In tribal areas however, no second crop is grown.

Share of By-Products

In the village Nalabanta where sugarcane is grown the entire product is sold to the cooperative sugar factory and therefore, the question of sharing the by-products in case of sugarcane does not arise. So we are left with straw, the only by-product. One important feature may be mentioned here i.e. the sharing of by-products (straw) in some cases is related to the sharing of a part of costs of production namely fertiliser. If costs of manure is shared then a larger share is generally demanded by the landlords. But in our sample we do not have any such cases.

To take the unirrigated areas first, we note that while in Bhalliamunda a dual system of sharing of by-products exists in the village Balarampur we notice that it is mostly shared on a 50/50 basis between the landlord and the lessee. In Bhalliamunda since the lease is generally of a fixed rent system, the landlords are entitled to get only the fixed rent. There are only three cases where the landlord gets 50 per cent of straw and in all these cases tenants are comparatively in a weaker position compared to the lessors. In Balarampur only in two cases, in one 75 per cent and in another, 33 per cent of by-products are shared by landlords. Here again we find that it is the relative resource status of tenants which probably determines such a system of sharing of by-products. While in the former case the landlord is a big landlord and a dominant party, in the latter case it is the lessor who is relatively in a weaker status. *Whether a tenant or a landlord it is always the dominant party which enjoys at the cost of the weaker one.*

In the irrigated areas similarly, we find that while in Attabira the landlords do not share any by-products since the entire lease system is on a fixed rent basis, in Lunahar we find that straw is being shared between landlords and tenants. In some cases 25 per cent of the by-products is shared by tenants whereas in some other the entire amount of by-products is taken by the landlord. Almost in all cases entire crop is carried to the landlord's house to be crushed because the landlord apprehends pilferation by the tenant and the tenant is not allowed to share any amount of straw. But in case of second crop straw is shared in the same proportion i.e. 25 per cent for the landlord and 75 per cent for the tenant.

In the cash crop area, there are six cases where by-products are entirely taken by the landlord, and in three cases 60 per cent of the straw is shared by the landlord. As we have stated already lessors in these cases are generally in the big and medium size class and belong to the upper castes and thus appear to be dominating the lease market. There is a single case where a fixed amount of by-products are gien i.e. 200 bundles of straw per acre, while in another case the tenant gives some amount of straw to the landlord though could not state in definite terms the amount of by-products that he gives. But however, it is negligible since he does not attach much importance to this.

In the tribal areas, we find two different systems of sharing of by-products. While in some cases 100 per cent by-products are taken by landlords generally the large landowners, in some other cases 50 per cent of the by-products are taken by lessors. But in Mendhakhia since the entire lease system is on fixed rent basis, the landlords in many cases do not share any by-products, but in 4 cases where lessors take 50 per cent of the by-product the lessors generally are better off in relation to their tenants.

Free and Unpaid Labour Services

As we have noticed varying conditions in crop-sharing arrangements and sharing of the by-products, we also notice differences in the other accompanying conditions like free labour services, gifts like fuel wood etc. offered by tenants. We have indicated earlier that our sample villages are mainly from the *zamindary* tracts of the state. The influence of the age old *zamindary* system still persists in these villages and we still find labour services to be demanded by landlords in the traditional manner, but to a lesser extent. The labour services are generally rendered by tenant whenever asked for by the landlord, but very often tenants themselves offer such labour services 'voluntarily' in order to keep the landlord in good humour so that they will not be evicted.

In tribal areas, we have two different classes of landlords — big landowners , and very small landowners. The landowners belonging to the former category only demand unpaid or underpaid labour services and it is always the small tenants who are more exploited in this regard. There was one case where the tenant supplies the daily vegetable requirements of the landlord, since the tenant is a vegetable grower. There are some cases where along with the free labour services the tenants are required to supply fuel wood. Sometimes, this is a condition attached to the lease. There is another case where the tenant is asked to supervise the other leased out plots, collect the rental produce from the lessees and take over to the landlord.

Demand for such labour services is very common in unirrigated villages in our sample. It is again the small tenants who are vulnerable to such exploitation and it is mostly the big landlords who demand such labour services. But there are considerable variations in the amount of labour services rendered. While in some cases it is demanded by the lessors as a condition with the lease in other cases it is reported as being rendered 'voluntarily', but not as a condition attached to the lease. Similarly, in case of fuel wood, we find some landlords demand free fuel wood to be delivered or instead ask for a cash equivalent. Thus it is a rigid condition accompanying the lease whereas in some other cases the tenants are supplying free fuel wood wherever asked for but not as a condition of lease.

In Balarampur almost all lessors retain a part of their holding to carry out self-cultivation. But in fact the plot of land is cultivated by tenants. The tenants have to supply own labour and bullock labour where seed and fertilisers are provided by the landlord. The entire produce, however, is appropriated by the landowner. The tenant does not get anything.

In the irrigated areas, however, there is a marked difference. In the Irritated Region I in all but two cases free labour services are rendered by tenants whereas in the Irrigated Region II it is not so. Region I was under the zamindary system earlier and similary Region II was under the Gountia system, a system similar to the *zamindary* system. Villages with such a background generally have the practice of unpaid voluntary labour services rendered by the tenants. But in this case there is a difference. While Irrigated Region II has entirely a fixed rent kind of tenancy, Irrigated Region I is still under a cropsharing system of tenancy. Generally under the share-cropping system of land tenure practice of free labour services is attached 'almost' as a condition with the lease, whereas under fixed rent system of land tenure it is almost absent. In Lunahar, therefore, barring a few cases, all other leases have a condition of free labour services whereas in the Region II such a condition does not exist.

Apart from labour services, there also exists a peculiar kind of payment made to the landowner and this practice is perhaps because of the influence of the *zamindari* system. In Lunahar there is a small tenant with an operational holding of 2.20 acres, who has leased in from a big landlord, a descendent of the *zamindar* family. The tenant pays 10 kg. of paddy to the landlord every day during the harvest to meet the cost of the landlord's visits to his field. The amount thus calculated (according to the number of visits) is deducted from tenant's share of paddy after the harvest. 'Gift' on ceremonial occasions are a common feature and almost works as a demand since the landlords expect these from tenants.

Except in two cases where the lessors are small landowners, all other landlords in Nalabanta demand free labour services. As stated earlier, this village consists of lessors who are mostly Brahmins and have reported themselves as traditionally landlords and in fact seem to dominate the lease market.

Thus we notice free labour services in most cases are demanded but in a varying degree. The extent and content of this important component of lease condition is difficult to be quantified. But we can observe the variation in degree to be almost systematically related to the relative socio-economic position of lessors and lessees. We may observe that small tenants leasing in land from bigger landlords are the most vulnerable ones and are exploited to the maximum. Tenants both of the pure and owner-tenant category operating with holdings of less than 5 acres are subjected to this sort of exploitation. Apart from the labour services, some provide free fuel wood where as some others offer 'gifts' or work in the landlord's fields free. The situation deteriorates further with the uncertainty in employment opportunity, competition in the lease market, and above all the threat of eviction that exists very prominently. In a situation like this the tenant has no option but to cling to the lease parcel, he is compelled to keep the landlord in good humour rather than to go without the lease.

Caste also plays a role in this condition of lease: we observe it is mostly lessees belonging to the lower castes of the society who are more prone to such exploitation. We have cases where the tenants are *Brahmins* (which is of course a rare phenomenon) who do not render any kind of labour service to their landlords. But they do supply fuel wood etc. to the landlord.

Lease Duration

Duration of the lease is an important element in the tenurial system. Whether share-cropping or fixed rent tenancy leases of short durations are expected to affect production adversely. A tenant might take more interest in cultivation in case the lease is of a longer duration, the tenant may undertake some capital investment the returns to which are expected only in the long run. We do not intend to bring in the controversy here as to what should be the ideal duration of the lease to yield maximum gains in production. What we intend to argue here is that in a land lease market where the basic norms of a competitive market are non-existent and where monopoly and monopsony conditions influence the entire lease market, the duration of the lease contract would naturally depend upon the motives of the landlord and the relative socio-economic status of the lessee.

We found that the large landlords and also the small landowners lease out land only for short durations. Whether it is share-cropping or fixed rent tenancy the lease is generally given for a very short duration i.e. one agricultural year. In some areas we find, the irrigated areas in particular, lease durations are limited to a single crop alone.

There is one possible factor which has influenced the lease durations. That is the impact of the land reform legislation in the post-independence period, particularly in the late 60s, when land legislations were aimed at the removal of the intermediaries. Apprehensive of losing land and rent thereof the landlords resorted to leasing out land only to those who are faithful, restricting lease duration only to a very short period. There are instances where landlords have continued with the same tenants but exchanged leased out plot among the tenants. This method, as expected by landlord, disallows the tenants from claiming occupancy rights over the tenanted land. Therefore, almost in all cases we find lease durations being limited to very short periods.

One particular factor needs to be mentioned here — when the leases are oral agreement[3] it is difficult to ascertain the duration of such leases. We obtained our information through a direct enquiry. We enquired from the tenants and the corresponding landlords as well and we observed that both reported that leases are mostly of very short durations and in many cases nothing definitely is known to tenants about the length of the lease period. The same tenants continue to cultivate the same leased in plots after the expiry of an agricultural year but it is always treated as though it were a new lease.

In cash crop area for example, we find that lease is given

for a short duration mostly for one year. It is not definite if the same tenant will continue to hold the lease as these leases are generally oral.

But in the irrigated villages in the Region I there are six cases out of thirteen where lease is given for an unspecified period. In these cases the tenatns have been cultivating under the same landlord but there have been changes in the plots or they have been cultivating with discontinuity with a gap of one year in between the leases. Therefore, the tenants remain doubtful of the lease period. In another six cases the lease is only for a single crop. There is one case where the lease is explicitly for a year only. In case of the summer paddy when the HYV is grown, leases cover generally for a single crop. But in the1990 because of repair work in the canal flow irrigation is not available. Pulses etc. are grown immediately after the kharif crop.

In the Irrigated Region II comprising Attabira, Paramanpur and Babebira we note that in almost all cases the lease is given for one year only. There are some cases where the lease is given for four or eight crops where the rent is already advanced for the total period in cash. This practice resorted to by some landlords is a recent phenomenon. In the 1990s the practice of rent being paid in cash still continues to exist. But in cases of fixed kind rent, the rent is paid in kind but immediately after harvest.

There are seven cases out of 26 observations in the unirrigated areas where the lease is given for an unspecified period; that is, the lease can be discontinued at any time the landlord desires. There are nine cases where duration of the lease is only for a year. We also observe similar number of cases where the leases is taken only for a single crop. This is particularly the case in village Balarampur where some tenants lease in land in the neighbouring village to grow HYV paddy.

In the tribal areas almost in all cases we notice that the lease is given for one agricultural year. The few cases where the leases are given for an unspecified period, the tenants generally continue to cultivate the same plot, but the lease is renewed every year. There are two cases where the lease is given for a period — more than two years.

One possible explanation for this short duration of the lease may be that the landlord tries to capitalise the productivity gains firstly by increasing the rent and secondly by reducing the lease duration to a very short period.[4]

In the Irrigated Region II, in the unirriated villages, and in case of tenants producing sugarcane in the cash crop area we notice that there exists a system of fixed rent. The strategy is this — fixed rent system of tenancy is supposed to give an incentive to tenants to maximise production through an intensive cultivation of the leased in land, since what remains after the payment of rent accrues to the tenant. But by making the lease contract short enough and/or insecure, the landlord can raise fixed rent and capitalise on the productivity gains for each new tenant or for the old tenant under a threat of eviction. This quick turn over of tenants, even when actually involving eviction, may not particularly harm productivity, if gains in productivity are mainly being achieved through the tenants circulating capital rather than through asset formation.[5]

Evictions

In 28 out of 120 cases in all these villages taken together tenants have reported explicit threats of eviction from landlords. Of the 28, in 13 cases the tenants have been evicted by force, large number of cases occuring in the tribal areas we have surveyed. Where evictions have been done through pressure we observe that in some cases they have been done through the court of law i.e. by legal force; but in majority of cases it is through physical force that the tenants have been evicted.

One factor, however, should not be ignored here, i.e. in our observations we have a large number of cases where the lease is given for a short duration generally for one agricultural year. Therefore, even though the threat of eviction has not been actually pronounced by the landlord, he still has the power to evict any tenant or discontinue the lease. We have mentioned earlier that all these are only oral agreements having no legal force behind the contract. As such tenants remain only tenants at will, i.e. the lease is terminable at any time. The tenants continue to cultivate only at the pleasure of the landlord. Thus even if eviction does not actually occur the tenants always have the fear of being evicted. Even the tenants who have been cultivating land leasing in from a particular landlord for some extended period are not free from such fear of being evicted at any time. The landlords' reactions to the recent land reform legislations is a major factor for creating such an uncertainty in the lease duration.

There are also some tenants who have reported to have surrendered the leased in land 'voluntarily'. But in fact leased in plots have been surrendered by tenants through indirect pressure. The tenants are left with no alternative but to surrender the leased in land because their weak socio-economic position does not allow them to take recourse to any legal help. In fact we have examples where the tenants have miserably failed in legal efforts and at last had to yield to landlord's desires.

Cost Sharing Arrangements of the Lease

Leases, where the cost of production is shared, are rare. Particularly, in cases where lease is given on fixed rent we observe costs are not being shared between the landlord and the tenant.

The cases where production costs are shared are largely seen in the irrigated village Lunahar, where tenants from the neighbouring village across the river used to lease in land in order to cultivate high yielding paddy under a cropsharing system (1974-75 survey). In this case, however, the lessors only bear half of the cost of fertiliser applied to land. This is done as the tenants (as reported by them) cannot bear the whole cost of fertiliser and other inputs applied to land.

But here again (as we have seen in the case of Irrigated Region II) the motive of landlords to appropriate the gains from the HYV paddy cultivation remains. In fact in a situation where the cost of inputs like fertilisers, labour and HYV seeds are high, and the tenant receives but a part of the gross produce under a crop sharing system, it may not be conducive for them to cultivate the leased in land intensively or the tenant might not be able to raise subsistence, he may relax his endeavours. The landlord, therefore, may ameliorate the situation by increasing the share of the tenant or share part of the cost as he does here. We find that here the landlords share half of the fertiliser cost and also allow a larger share, 75 per cent of the gross produce to the tenant. Thus they provide an incentive to the tenant to maximise his efforts to raise productivity. But gradually the landlords try to increase their own share of the gross produce. In fact as reported by tenants, the landlord's share of the gross produce had recently gone up from 20 to the present 25 per cent of the gross produce. Therefore, even though the cost is shared it is but a marginal proportion of the total cost and the landlord has not failed to extract the maximum in the given circumstances.

In the unirrigated regions, there is no sharing of costs except in two cases where cost of seeds are shared, one where the land is leased out on a fixed rent and in the other the landlord stipulates the crop, but however, this did not alter the crop sharing arrangements since the loans were repaid back after the harvest. The cost of inputs are borne entirely by tenants in the cash crop area except two cases. In one case, the landlord shared the cost of inputs 'partly' and increased his share of the gross produce by 15 per cent more. In the other case, the landlord shared the water charges but the share-cropping arrangements however, remained unchanged.

Landlords Stipulating Crop

We do not have many cases where the landlords have stipulated the crop. This is largely because of the limitations of alternative crops to be grown. For example, in both the irrigated regions generally paddy is grown. Because of the flooding system of irrigation it is mostly not possible to grow other crops. Moreover HYV paddy is supposed to yield more. In the unirrigated areas, it is the scarcity of water which is largely responsible for landlords not stipulating the crop.

Thus, there are only a few cases in these areas where we find landlords stipulating the crop. In tribal area we find landlords stipulating the crop, one amongst them stipulating HYV to be grown. In the cash crop area we find the maximum frequency of landlords stipulating for the cultivation of cash crop namely sugarcane. There are 8 out of 25 cases where the tenants have reported this.

In case of Balarampur (which did not have any irrigation facilities in 1974), there are landlords who stipulate particular crop to be produced in the leased out land parcels. Balrampur now in 90s has the lift irrigation facilities. As has been said earlier there is a complete transition in the agrarian situation. Through out the year the land is utilised for production of different crops either paddy or vegetables. The productivity of land has increased. Money wise the landlords and tenants have gained. The landowners who lease out land stipulate the particular crop to be produced in their leased out parcels of land. If the tenant is poor and is unable to cultivate vegetables (which is more paying because the yield is more) the landlord advances some credit for the purchase of different factor inputs. The tenant is thus induced to cultivate that particular crop which the landlord desires. The decision with regard to sharing of output rests with the lessor. The economically poor tenant agrees to the terms decided by the landlord.

Changes in the Mode and Amount of Rent Payment

We have collected information with regard to changes in rent paid, in terms of share or in terms of fixed rent, and the mode of rent payment. Earlier in this chapter we have given the details concerning the amount of share and fixed rent paid with regard to the major and minor crops and the by- products as well. But here we want to record briefly some recent changes, which are worth noting.

To take the cash crop area first, we find that out of 25, 18 tenants have reported an increase in the rent paid to landowners. In two cases tenants have reported that mode of payment has changed from share to fixed rents paid in terms of cash.

The most notable change is seen to have taken place in the irrigated areas particularly in Region II where there is a complete transition from share-cropping to fixed kind/cash system of tenancy. In the recent past the fixed kind rent is being replaced by fixed cash rent paid usually in advance. In the Irrigated Region I we notice all the tenants who were cultivating the high yielding variety paddy during the summer now pay a larger share, which has gone up from 20 to 25 per cent of the gross produce.

In village Balarampur in the 90s there is a change in the mode of rent payment and the cropping pattern. Now paddy apart, different types of vegetables are grown because of availability of lift irrigation facilities. The productivity of land has increased. Therefore, the lessors have tried to manoeuvre the mode of rent payment in their favour. While for paddy the lease is given on crop sharing basis for vegetables the land parcels are leased out on fixed rent. When it is crop sharing, the total gross produce is shared on 50/50 basis while for fixed rent it comes to about 65/35, 65 per cent being appropriated by the lessor. (This we get when we impute the fixed rent in relation to gross output produced by the tenant). The landlords find it more profitable and quite often induce the tenant by advancing some credit to cultivate the stipulated crop. What is more is the free labour services rendered by the tenant besides the rent paid for the leased in land.

In tribal and in the unirrigated area there are only 3 and 2 cases respectively where the tenants have reported paying an increased share which has gone up in the recent years.

In spite of the rent regulations through land reform legislations, we find the landlord's share to be gradually increasing which speaks of the fact that the landlords wield more bargaining power in the land-lease market and their comparatively better socio-economic position helps them to have a favourable bargaining strength.

REFERENCES

1. There has been a remarkable change in the case of one tenant who admitted this. They are two brothers who are engaged in agriculture. Though they own a small parcel of land major portion of their operational holding is land leased in from two landlords of the village. His economic status has improved. His thatched house gives a different look and he has already constructed two rooms with concrete roof. Perhaps the improved economic status has given him the self-confidence.
2. This is a small tenant, who had been cultivating a leased in plot from a comparatively big landlord of the village. The tenant wanted to establish his occupancy right on the land (leased in). Aprehending this the landlord tried to evict the tenant. The tenant sought legal protection. The case was tried in the High Court where the tenant lost. The tenant lost whatever property he had. Therefore, to eke out a living, he has no other option but to seek leases at whatever terms and conditions laid down by the landlords.
3. In most cases land parcels are leased out under oral agreement. The lessors do not put this in a written form because such an agreement may lead to legal complications. Under the land reform legislation tenancy is completely prohibited. In some areas we were informed by the tenant farmers that he is not a lessee but only a wage earner engaged in the field. This he

gives in writing or signs in an agreement from. Such a document indeed helps the lessor to evade the impact of land reform legislation where tenancy is completely prohibited. See Das P.K. Some aspects of tenancy in Orissa — A case Study of Sambalpur and Cuttack, districts M.Phil, dissertation (unpublished) J.N.U., New Delhi, 1973.

4. This explanation was offered in Krishna Bharadwaj; *Production Conditions in Indian Agriculture*, (Cambridge University Press, 1974) pp. 53-55.
5. Krishna Bharadwaj and P.K. Das, "Tenurial Conditions and Mode of Exploitation ... etc." op.cit.

6

AGRARIAN TRANSITION IN VILLAGE ATTABIRA

We have made an in-depth study of the Irrigated Region II particularly the village Attabira where we notice a complete shift in the tenancy system — a transition from share-cropping arrangement to a fixed rent system and gradually changing over to fixed cash rent system of land tenure and finally to a system where the cash rent is paid in advance at the time when the lease is taken. The transition has occurred because of the introduction of canal irrigation along with the cultivation of the HYV paddy. It is worth investigating the gradual shift in the land tenure system and its impact on the lease pattern and lease terms and conditions. The initial survey was done during the year 1975 and most of the findings are based on the information collected during that year. In the 90s, the second round of the survey was undertaken to find what changes have taken place over the period. The findings of both the survey are quite revealing and interesting, too.

Attabira consists of the main village Attabira and two hamlets — Bhallupalli and Beiman Tikra situated on its either side. The agrarian conditions of the village have undergone considerable changes since the late 60s with the introduction of the irrigation facilities and the advent of the Green Revolution. We carried out an intensive survey of all the households engaged in either leasing out or leasing in, the agro-economic structure of the village in order to find out the transition in agrarian relations.

Introductory Background

A few decades ago the village did not enjoy economic importance in spite of its locational advantage. The village is situated on the National Highway and is only 30 KM far from the headquarters of Sambalpur district. It did not have any irrigation facilities and was only a monocropping region with traditional pattern of cultivation followed in the village. But at present, it has acquired an important position in the region as it has experienced significant improvement in its agro-economic conditions. The cropping pattern has changed; consumption of fertilisers has gone up; the per acre yield has increased considerably. Population has increased in recent years and especially of the immigrants who constitute a significant proportion of the total population of the village. The area being a double cropping region, there is a large influx of tenant farmers from Andhra Pradesh. Similarly, there has been a steady demand for labourers and as such a considerable number of labour families have immigrated and settled down in the village. The most notable features of the village are:

(i) The increase in the number of agricultural labourers from 117 to 466. This might be largely due to the increased demand for such labourers all through the year.

(ii) The increase in the scheduled caste population, largely engaged in agricultural operations. Most of this scheduled caste population constitutes immigrants who have settled down in the village because of increasing opportunities of agricultural employment.

(iii) We also note a considerable decrease in the number of cultivators. This may be partly due to the tenants being recorded as agricultural labourers following land reforms legislation. In fact, prior to 1955 and the enactment of Orissa

Tenants' Protection and Relief Act, this part of the state did not experience any major land legislation. Consequently most of the tenants might have been recorded as 'cultivators'. But after 1965 with more amendments to the Act of 1955 landlords have probably more conscious of the potential threat of tenants claiming their rights. This might have led to manipulation of records. Secondly there may have been also genuine loss of land.

In order to bring out the changes that have taken place over the period we compared the findings of the Farm Management Studies with those of our field survey and again the resurvey that we have done in the 90s. According to the FMS (the FMS study was based on a sample survey), during the period 1957-59, as many as 108 out of 167 households in the village were engaged in cultivation i.e. 62.43 per cent of the families were engaged in the primary sector of the economy. Agriculture was the major source of their livelihood and families engaged in activities other than agriculture were negligible. The families engaged as labourers also constituted a significant proportion and out of 173, 56 i.e. 32.37 per cent of families were seen to have been working as labourers. This includes labourers engaged in various categories of work. But job opportunities being limited a large proportion remained engaged in cultivation.

Compared to these, we have the following figures of the village for the year 1975. We have done a complete enumeration of the village and have classified the families (not households; there are households where more than one family have been living jointly) according to their main occupation.

Table 6.1 shows that out of 817 families, 290 families are engaged in agricultural operations. These include the landlords (who do not actively participate the operational work), owner cultivators-cum-landlords (those who cultivate their owned holdings and lease out a part to be cultivated by tenants) owner

TABLE : 6.1

Distribution of Households engaged in Leasing-in or Leasing-out

No. of Families	Total No. of Families	Landlords	Owner Cultivators-Cum-Landlords	Owner Cultivators	Owner Tenants	Pure Tenants	Wage Labour of all Categories (Except Attached Labourers)	Attached Labourers	Service	Business	Others
1975	817	44	2	179	20	8	322	37	79	99	27
		(5.36)	(0.24)	(21.85)	(2.45)	(0.98)	(40.0)	(4.40)	(9.51)	(12.00)	(3.25)
1990	928	50	2	213	20	7	369	48	85	107	27
		(5.38)	(0.21)	(20.95)	(2.15)	(0.75)	(39.76)	(5.17)	(9.15)	(11.63)	(2.90)

Note: Figures in the parenthesis are the percentage of Households to the total.

cultivators, owner tenants—where the operational holdings include their owned holding plus leased - in land, pure tenants where the operational holding consists of only the leased - in land. Here we have excluded the wage labourers. But of the 322 labour families more than 77 per cent i.e. 249 labour families are engaged in agricultural operations. Although the FMS and our survey data are not strictly comparable, we may note that, compared to the FMS figures, there has been an increase in the category of daily wage earners.

Cropping Pattern: Earlier to 1960, when cultivation of crops was entirely dependent upon the monsoon, only a single crop, mainly paddy, was being cultivated. Large tracts of land were left fallow. These were mainly the up lands called as *Att* land and were of poor fertility. This apart there are three other different types of land, *Mal*, *Bahal* and *Berna* lands. *Mal* land is comparatively better than the *Att* land. The other two types of land *Bahal* and *Berna* are low lands and lie at the depression of slopes and were considered to be the most fertile lands. These two categories of land could yield a second crop even when irrigation facilities were not extended to the area.

With the introduction of canal irrigation most of the areas in the village enjoy canal irrigated water all through the year. The water shade area comprises a large part of the village Beiman Tikra,[1] one of the two hamlets of the village Attabira. The other hamlet Bhalupalli however, has the full advantage of irrigation while the main village Attabira has lands belonging to both categories. Even now there are some areas (in Beiman Tikra) which are monocropped while the rest are double cropped.

In the 60s, the cultivable area in the village increased considerably. Prior to 1960, only 963.66 acres were cultivable producing only a single crop. According to the revenue[2] records the total area 2538.10 acres (which includes cultivable lands and waste lands also) 80 per cent of the land has been made cultivable;

77 per cent of the total land has been brought under irrigation and is double cropped. The revenue records also show that while 1836.40 acres has been cultivated during the *kharif*, 1561.96 acres are being cultivated during the *rabi* season.

Paddy is largely grown both in the *kharif* and in the *rabi* seasons. During the *kharif* generally the ordinary variety of paddy is grown, whereas during *rabi* only the HYV paddy is cultivated. In the up-land oil seeds are grown after paddy. But adoption of HYV paddy cultivation was not immediate but very gradual since the response both by tenants and owner cultivators was rather poor. We will discuss this in greater detail later.

Following the classification of families in respect to their main occupation we find (See Table 6.1) about 31 per cent of the total number of families have interest in land as cultivators or as lessors of land. This of course excludes the agricultural labourers who infact constitute about 45 per cent of the total labour families engaged in agriculture. Thus, including the agricultural labour families more than 76 per cent of the families of the village Attabira are involved directly or indirectly in this primary sector. There are 181 owner cultivators out of whom 2 partially lease out land only for a short period. About 21.9 per cent of the total households are owner cultivators. In the village, about 3.50 per cent of households are tenants which include both owner-tenants and pure tenants. But the number of owner-tenants is higher than that of the pure tenants.

There are 44 lessors i.e. 5.36 per cent of the total households leasing out to lessees living in this village and in the neighbouring villages. Among the lessors we find both small as well as big landlords. The motivational factors influencing leasing out differ. With the adoption of HYV paddy cultivation, the lessors particularly big landlords lease out because it is considered to be more lucrative, while the small land owners owning less than two acres of land do so because they find it difficult to undertake self-cultivation either because of lack of finance or because of lack of manpower in the family. The latter class of 'landlords' seem to have increased in the recent past, particularly since the early 70s.

We have recorded the changes in the operational holding that have occurred since 1965 in order to observe the effect of irrigation on the economic condition of families (depending largely on agriculture) represented mainly through their operational holding or the ownership holding. So far as the lessors are concerned we do not find significant changes in their ownership holding. Out of the 18 landlords that we have covered in the survey in all cases except one, the ownership holding has remained unchanged since 1964. The only case that we have referred to, the landlord has sold 10 acres of land and now possesses only four and half acres, of which 2 acres have been mortgaged with the money lender.

In the case of owner cultivators, we find considerable changes in the operational holding. Out of 45 owner cultivators in the sample, in 7 cases the operational holding has become smaller. The reasons are many — it might either be due to sale of land, or partition of the joint family or due to the fact that the owner-cultivator has ceased to lease in. There are another 7 cases where the operational holding has increased. In all these cases the increase in the operational holding is due to purchase of more land. In three cases the addition to the owned holdings has been significant and in one case as much as 12 acres of land have been purchased in the last ten years period. Except these 14 cases, in the rest of the cases the ownership holding have remained unaltered.

In case of wage earners, we find only a single case where the labourer has acquired 2 acres of land given to him by the Government in the process of distribution of land to landless labourers. Out of 60, in 14 cases the entire owned holding or part of it has been sold or lost to money lender for non-repayment of loans. The loans were incurred largely to meet their consumption needs. These wage labourers have been compelled to become daily wage earners because of their weak economic position.

The operational holding of tenants have changed in twenty-five cases while it has remained the same in the rest three cases. In 12 cases, the operational holdings show an increase while in 11 cases it had decreased and there is a single case where the tenant is a fresh lease holder. In 9 cases, the tenants were earlier only owner cultivators and were not leasing in, but with the introduction of perennial irrigation and crops being more or less assured they have started leasing in. In a single case, the tenant stated that the necessity to lease in land arose because he had sold out a part of his land in order to meet his consumption needs.

Thus, we find the ownership or operational holdings have changed considerably in cases of owner-cultivators, tenants and wage earners whereas landlords' (lessors') holdings have remained more or less unchanged.

Transition to HYV

We have stated earlier that HYV cultivation was very gradually adopted. One of the reasons that can be stated for this is the risk involved in the adoption of HYV cultivation. The initiative was therefore, taken by the government, which however, had little impact initially on the farmers of this village. It was only after a decade that the local cultivators started availing of the irrigated water which was introduced in the area already in 60s. The migrant tenant farmers were the early cultivators of HYV in the village. The irrigation facilities and relatively low rents on leased out land were the main attractions for some Andhra cultivators to immigrate to this village.[3]

The immigrant tenant cultivators could gain maximum from the leased in plots because of low rent. Perhaps this induced some farmers to adopt HYV and a few cultivators started cultivating it but in the traditional pattern, they did not use adequate fertilisers, nor adopted other measures to prevent pest attacks and consequently the yield was poor. Moreover, in the 1969 there was a heavy damage to the crop due to pest attack. These were some of the important factors to discourage the local farmers from adoption of HYV cultivation. It was only in the early 70s that HYV came to cultivated on a large scale. In the *kharif* season however, ordinary paddy used to be sown till 1974 when some farmers started growing HYV. The low adoption of HYV as a *kharif* crop is largely due to the fear of pests which is very common during the *kharif* season because of the damp soil and lack of sunshine which helps the pests to multiply. The breeding season of Gall Midges being the months of August and September, the *kharif* crop is more vulnerable to this kind of pest attack.[4]

Who Adopts

The main impetus behind the adoption of HYV cultivation by the local farmers was the large output harvested by the immigrant tenant farmers. Among the local farmers some of the tenant first started cultivating HYV. The tenant farmers felt more urgently the need to cultivate HYV in order to enable themselves to pay the higher rents demanded by the lessors (higher rents were demanded by lessors as a result of the increased production on some of the leased out land). We can find that all except two of the tenants surveyed started cultivating HYV in the 1969 which however, remained confined to the *rabi* season alone while during the *kharif* season all tenant farmers except one have been cultivating ordinary paddy.

The case of owner cultivators, however, is different. The change from ordinary to HYV cultivation was relatively slow. In fact till 1969 only a few i.e. 10 out of 45 owner-cultivators surveyed were seen to be cultivating HYV. Rest of the owner cultivators started cultivating HYV in the early 70s. The gradual adoption of HYV may possibly be because of the risk involved.

One difference was noticed between the owner- cultivators and the tenant farmers; that is, in the case of the latter, cultivation of HYV during the *kharif* season was rarely seen whereas a comparatively larger number of owner-cultivators were seen to be cultivating HYV in both seasons. (while among the tenant cultivators only one was cultivating HYV, in the case of owner-cultivators as many as 10 were growing HYV, during the *kharif* season. This, however, was but a small proportion of the total number of cultivators).

Another notable factor is that the operational holding of a farmer whether tenant or owner-cultivator, does not show clearly any relationship with the adoption of HYV cultivation. But we may roughly say, from what we find in our sample that the small cultivators were the early adopters of HYV. There are a number of factors which may be working towards the small tenants adopting HYV. Firstly, the lease may be, and frequently is, conditional upon the cultivation of HYV. Secondly, the high fixed rents as well as insecurity of lease pressurises the tenant to adopting HYV in order to increase gross productivity of the cultivated plot. Thirdly, the need to raise as much of subsistence as possible on the small plot of land under cultivation may induce small farmers as well as tenants to adopt HYV.

In 1969 a large number of tenant and owner-cultivators started cultivating the HYV. But because of unfavourable conditions particularly the pest attack, the crop was badly damaged and the yield was very poor. This was mainly the reason for which for three successive years cultivation of HYV was discontinued.

Use of Better Seeds

Since 1972 HYV is widely cultivated particularly during the *rabi* season and in the *kharif*, ordinary paddy continues to be cultivated. Since 1974 some owner and tenant cultivators switched over to cultivating the HYV even during the *kharif* season. This is considered to be risky because the cultivation of HYV during the *kharif* season, as noted already, is more vulnerable to pest attack.

TABLE : 6.2

Input Structure of Tenanted Holdings in Different Size Groups

Sl. No. of Tenant	*Amount of land Leased in*	*Total Operational Holding*	*Costs of Other Inpute Per Acre*	*Cost of Fertiliser Inputs (Per Acre)*		*Total Cost (Per Acre)*		*Total Cost*	*Amount of Paddy Harvested (Total)*	*Interest Charges*		*Net Y Without Deducting Rent Paid*	*Net Y* Per Acre Without Duducting Rent Paid*
				Ordinary	*HYV*	*Ordinary*	*HYV*			*Co.op.Soc.*	*Money Lenders*		
1	*2*	*3*	*4*	*5*	*6*	*7*	*8*	*9*	*10*	*11*	*12*	*13*	*14*
2	2.00	2.00	300	200	385	500	685	2370	6480	-	860	3750	937.50
1	4.00	4.00	240	200	300	440	540	3920	10240	-	-	6320	790.00
4	4.00	4.00	310	224	256	534	566	4400	9920	-	216	5304	663.00
5	4.50	4.50	305	220	390	525	695	5490	11920	-	-	6230	692.22
6	2.50	4.50	315	200	370	515	685	5400	12960	-	200	7360	817.77
8	5.00	6.50	270	115	275	385	545	6045	10000	312	1080	2563	197.15
9	3.00	3.65	200	200	410	400	610	3687	9120	54	75	5304	726.57
10	2.00	6.50	240	200	385	440	625	6922	17200	-	90	10188	783.69
11	2.00	5.00	290	200	350	490	640	5650	10400	18	-	4732	473.20
15	4.00	8.00	320 330-R	200	415	520	745	10120	19840	164	-	9556	597.25
16	3.00	5.00	305	200	390	505	695	6000	14400	102	-	8298	829.80
17	3.00	6.00	310 330-R	200	385	510	715	7350	16800	153	-	9297	774.75
18	2.50	5.00	305 310-R	250	420	555	730	6425	14400	102	-	7873	787.30
19	4.00	7.00	310 320-R	250	400	550	720	8960	17760	102	-	8698	621.28

Contd/-.

TABLE : 6.2 (Contd.)

1	2	3	4	5	6	7	8	9	10	11	12	13	14
20	4.50	8.00	300	200	410	500	720	9760	15360	153	-	6147	384.18
			310-R										
21	4.00	7.00	325	215	425	540	750	9030	16240	127	-	7083	505.92
22	4.50	7.00	305	200	390	505	695	8400	17920	153	-	9367	669.07
26	4.00	7.20	305	200	400	505	710	8748	15600	102	100	6650	461.80
			310-R										
27	4.00	5.50	315	200	420	515	745	6930	12400	102	-	5368	488.00
			325-R										
3	9.50	9.50	300	180	295	480	595	10213	20240	-	360	9667	508.78
7	3.50	11.50	276	150	370	426	646	12328	21430	225	-	8877	385.95
12	8.00	16.00	275	215	400	490	685	14690	25200	156	-	10354	398.23
		10.00-R	285-R										
13	3.50	10.00	273	200	450	473	733	12060	23200	165	-	10975	548.75
			283-R										
14	15.00	17.00	272	200	400	472	672	19448	36480	153	360	16519	485.85
23	4.00	10.00	325	250	400	575	740	13150	24480	204	-	11126	556.30
			340-R										
24	4.00	9.00	295	200	398	495	703	10782	18720	153	-	7785	432.50
			305-R										
25	6.00	9.00	305	190	380	495	695	10710	20880	153	100	9917	550.94
			315-R										

* Net income here means total income minus cost of other inputs, cost of fertiliser, and interest charges on loans if any.

TABLE : 6.3

Input Structure of Owned Holdings in Different Size Groups

Sl. No.	Operational Holding	Costs of Inputs Other Than Fertiliser	Cost of Fertiliser		Total Cost Per Acre		Total Cost for the Operational Holding in a Year	Amount Harvested (Total)	Interests Paid on Loans from All Sources.	Net* Income	Net Income Per Acre
			Ordinary	HYV	Ordinary	HYV					
1	2	3	4	5	6	7	8	9	10	11	12
6	2.50	296	200	200	496	496	2480	4960	30	2450	490.00
7	3.00	285	Nil	300	285	585	2610	4320	-	1710	285.00
8	3.00	370	170	270	540	640	3540	8000	80	4380	730.00
11	2.00	305	200	250	505	555	2120	4160	390	2650	662.50
15	1.50	302	150	300	452	602	1581	2800	-	1219	406.33
17	2.00	265	200	300	465	565	2060	3680	30	1590	397.50
20	3.00	262/270	232	350	494	620	3342	8000	60	4598	766.33
30	3.00	265	300	400	565	665	3690	7920	78	4152	692.00
36	1.00	240	10	10	250	250	500	800	-	300	150.00
37	3.00	255	150	350	405	505	3030	8000	144	4326	804.33
41	1.70	290	100	200	390	490	1496	3360	36	1840	541.18
43	1.00	245	Nil	Nil	245	245	490	560	-	70	35.00
44	3.00	295	200	380	495	675	3510	8400	63	4827	804.50
9	4.00										
	2.00R	322	300	400	622	722	3932	8800	50	4858	809.67
13	2.50	280	100	200	380	480	1430	2800	102	1268	362.29
	1.00R										

Contd.\-

TABLE : 6.3 (Contd.)

1	2	3	4	5	6	7	8	9	10	11	12
14	4.00	300	100	150	400	450	2500	1600	360	— 900	— 150
	2.00R										
16	3.50	295	86	248	381	271	1467	1440	6	— 33	— 8.25
	.50R										
18	5.00	295	160	250	455	545	5000	12800	60	7740	774.0
19	6.00	295	100	175	395	470	5190	12000	63	6747	562.25
22	7.00	390	204	398	594	728	9674	16800	-	7126	509.00
25	4.00	290/310	200	400	490	710	4800	7600	72	2728	341.00
26	4.50	300	200	300	500	600	4950	9200	158	4092	454.67
28	2.50	300	300	400	600	700	2900	5600	84	2616	581.33
	2.00R										
29	4.50	320	200	325	520	645	3952	5440	90	1198	171.14
	2.50R										
31	8.00	280	120	200	400	480	7040	20400	90	13270	829.38
33	8.00	280	120	250	400	530	7440	16000	120	8440	527.50
38	8.00	315	280	320	595	635	9840	16160	150	6170	385.63
40	5.00	275	-	324	275	599	4370	7200	60	2770	277.00
42	4.50	295	100	200	395	495	4005	6800	48	2747	305.22
45	7.50	300	200	385	500	685	8887	20000	42	11070.50	738.03
1	10.00	318	250	420	568	738	13060	30000	240	16700	835.00
2	15.00	315	250	410	565	725	19350	44400	360	24690	823.00
3	9.50	355	250	407	605	762	12986	28400	210	15204	800.19
4	10.00	345	200	450	545	795	13400	32000	270	18330	916.50
5	13.00	326	200	420	562	746	14766	22080	300	7014	304.96
	10.00R										

10	9.00 5.00R	315	300	400	615	715	9110	18400	120	9170	655.00
12	11.00 8.00R	320	200	400	520	720	11480	17200	192	5528	290.95
21	15.00 7.00	350	200	400	550	750	13500	44000	240	30260	1375.45
23	10.00	280	100	280	380	560	9400	28800	268	19132	956.60
24	10.00	350	165	350	515	700	12150	32000	222	19628	981.40
27	10.50 8.00R	300	300	450	600	750	12300	26000	240	13460	727.57
32	9.00	265	250	450	515	715	11070	22400	405	10925	606.94
34	13.00	270	150	250	420	520	12220	23200	600	10380	399.23
35	10.00	295	150	250	445	545	9900	24000	150	13950	697.50
39	8.50	330	250	300	580	630	10285	15200	144	4771	280.65

*** Net income here means total minus cost of inputs other than fertiliser, cost of fertiliser and interest paid on loan if any.**

But the '*Jagannath*' variety of paddy which is considered to be more pest resistant has induced the cultivator to grow HYV during the *kharif* season.

Use of Fertiliser

Application of fertiliser is usually less for *kharif* paddy since ordinary paddy does not need so much of feltiliser and secondly, the investment of fertiliser may be a waste if weather conditions are not favourable. But for the *rabi* crop, investment on fertiliser is comparatively much higher since yield of HYV largely depend upon the application of fertiliser. Therefore, we notice that barring a few cases all tenants as well as owner-cultivators apply considerable amount of fertiliser for the HYV cultivated during the *rabi* season.

One notable factor which needs to be mentioned here is that while all tenant cultivators use considerable amount of fertiliser the owner-cultivators particularly with small sized operational holding appear to be applying less than the amount of fertiliser required per acre. On an average, we find that while the tenant cultivators apply fertiliser worth Rs 380/- per acre of *rabi* HYV crop the owner cultivators apply on an average, fertiliser worth Rs 202/- (See Table 6.2 and 6.3). Similarly for the *kharif* paddy, we also note the tenant cultivators to be utilising more of fertiliser i.e. of Rs 305/- per acre whereas the owner-cultivators use it to the extent of Rs 175/-. This, on the face of it, appears to contradict the usual presumptions concerning input use on owned and tenanted lands. In order to distinguish, the pattern of use of fertiliser among the various tenants we plotted a scatter diagram wherein, along the abscissa was recorded the proportion of area leased in and on the vertical axis the per acre investment of fertiliser. We did not find any strong association between the two but as the proportion of leased-in area increased the per acre fertiliser investment slightly increased continuing upto a point where the proportion of leased-in land constituted a little above 56 per cent of the total operational holding, and thereafter slightly declined. Tenants who do not own land and cultivate only the leased-in land were seen to be investing less of fertiliser per acre generally. These remarks however, are to be interpreted extremely cautiously as the tendencies were too weak to support any generalisation. So far as the owner-cultivators are concerned we also plotted a similar scatter diagram (relating fertiliser use per acre to size of operational holding) and found no clear association between the two.

Similarly, exercises relating total investments (includes cost of fertiliser, bullock labour, human labour, pesticides and interest paid for credits if any) to percentage area leased in failed to reveal any definite or consistent association. In the case of owner-cultivators, we found that total investment per acre slightly increased with increase in the size of operational holding. Our observations are thus in conformity with the findings of other researchers into effects of tenancy referred to earlier. We may recall our comments there on the weaknesses of using percentage of area leased in as an explanatory variable.

Use of Mechanical Implements

Till recently various agricultural operations were being done by human and bullock labour. But since 1972 tractors are being used for ploughing the field. Both tenants as well as owner cultivators were seen to be hiring tractors for this purpose. More recently tractors are also being used for purposes of harvesting paddy. This is done because use of tractors can do the work more quickly. The cost of harvesting paddy by means of tractors does not differ much from that of using bullock labour. However, the small cultivators still use bullock labour for this purpose.

Gains from HYV Cultivation

The average output per acre has considerably increased

with the introduction of HYV and with improved farming practices. Prior to the introduction of irrigation only one crop was being produced in the village, paddy in the *kharif* season. Per acre capital investment was low. The average cost of all inputs per acre was only Rs 105/- and in the case of large operational holding the investment in inputs used to be Rs 99/- per acre which is lower than the average per acre inputs of Rs 125/- in the size group of 00.01 to 2.50 acres. Thus the level of investment was inadequate and this is not unexpected in a backward agrarian economy characterised by traditional agricultural practices and paucity of material and technical resources.[5] During 1957-60, the FMS notes, '38 per cent of the farms use inputs which is not worth more than Rs 100/- per acre. There is hardly a single farm which invests in inputs of more than Rs 250/- per acre. The majority of the farms concentrated in the size group of Rs 101/- to Rs 125/ - per acre.'[6] This is largely because of the risk involved in paddy cultivation due to complete dependence on the vagaries of monsoon. Low per acre investments and traditional methods of cultivation resulted in low per acre productivity. The FMS shows that "nearly three fourth of the farms yield an output which comes out to be not more than Rs 150/- per acre."[7]

Prior to the adoption of HYV with improved technology, chemical fertiliser were entirely absent in the input structure of the cultivating units. About a little more than a decade ago human labour was by far the most important item and accounted for 38 per cent of the total cost of inputs.[8] This overwhelming percentage of input of human labour alone reflects the primitive nature of farm practices. Bullock labour comes second in order of importance and accounts for about 20 per cent of the total input.[9] Compared to this in the present day break up of input structure, cost of fertiliser constitutes the major item followed by the expenditure on labour (both hired and family labour).[10] Next to this comes the bullock labour, both owned and hired. (For the sake of convenience we have included both bullock and human labour together and made it a single item in the cost structure shown in Tables 6.3 and 6.4. Other items like interest on credit availed of for operational expenses have been calculated separately and the cost structure of owner cultivated farms and tenant cultivated farms is given separately in order to study their comparative efficiency). All these costs have been deducted from the gross output in order to calculate the net income per acre.

In order to study the comparative efficiency, we have tried to relate the net income per acre (on the vertical axis) for the operational holding (on the abscissa). The tenant operated farms are clustered between 3-10 acre size holdings. In the case of tenant farmers we note that larger size holdings, particularly above 7 acres size group, in general, show low net income per acre compared to operational holdings with less than seven acres. Amongst the relatively smaller sized holdings net income per acre between the tenanted and owner cultivated holding does not differ much with tenanted holdings enjoying a slightly better position....[11]

It would seem, therefore, that the proportion of leased in land is less significant than the size of tenanted holding in explaining input use and productivity differentials. We may refer here to the observation made earlier that the higher intensity of farming and higher productivity on smaller holdings, whether tenanted or owned, arises due to the need for raising subsistence requirements.

Situation in the 90s however is different. In respect of costs of factor inputs like fertiliser, labour, pesticides etc. have gone up considerably. Besides this per acre rent has also gone up. The tenants have to face similar hardships — bearing higher costs of inputs, higher amount of rent and above all to eka out a living from the leased in land.

Conditions of Lease

Conditions Prior to 1960: The problem of tenancy was

not of much significance in the area about a couple of decades ago and the magnitude of tenancy was small. Table 6.4 would give us some idea about the land tenure situation in the village during the period preceding 1960; to be precise, during 1957-59.

One significant factor is that lease under fixed cash rent was conspicuously absent in the village, during this period. It is not only the leasing out pattern and the mode of rent payment but also the amount of rent paid to the lessor which needs to be noted here. During the period as the FMS figures show, that the amount of rent paid to the lessors works out to be Rs 17.21 per acre land leased out under crop-sharing tenancy whereas under fixed kind system of lease it turns out to be Rs 33.33 per acre.[12] Thus the per acre rental value was low which might be largely due to the low productivity of land.

After 1960

The picture in the post 1960 period has completely changed with the influx of tenant farmers from outside, facilities of irrigation and the advent of green revolution increasing the demand for land. The per acre productivity increased because of the adoption of HYV and this induced the lessors to raise the per acre rent. A tendency seemed to have developed among the lessors to lease out land for a fixed period of time with fixed rent payable to the lessor, largely because the lessors were interested in enhancing the rent in order to capitalise the gains of increased productivity.[13] Fresh lease was given only at an enhanced rent. Old tenants were allowed to continue if they agreed to pay the enhanced rent or were evicted and the lease was given to a fresh tenant. The lessor could increase the per acre rent by reducing the lease duration terminable at any time according to his pleasure thus increasing the insecurity of lease for the tenant.[14] Thus, we note not only a signijficant increase in the amount of rent per acre but also the insecurity of tenure.

TABLE : 6.4

	Owned and Self-Cultivated	*Taken Lease*				*Others*	*Total*
		Under Fixed Cash System	*Under Fixed Kind System*	*Crop sharing System*	*Total*		
Area in Acres	919.57	-	19.00	25.09	44.09	310.16	1282.82
Percentage to the Total	71.68	-	1.48	1.96	3.44	23.84	100.00

* Source: *Farm Management Studies*, (Sambalpur District) 1960, op.cit. P.177.

TABLE : 6.5

Amount of Rent and Mode of Rent Payment and the Relative Resource Position of Lessees and Lessors

Sl. No of Tenant	*Operational Holding*			*Status of the Landlord*	*Change in the Kind Rent*			*Changes in the Cash Rent*		*Change Over From Kind to Cash Rent*	
	Land Owned	*Land Leased-in*	*Total*		*1974*	*1975*	*Money Equivalent*	*1974*	*1975*	*1974*	*1975*
1	*2*	*3*	*4*	*5*	*6*	*7*	*8*	*9*	*10*	*11*	*12*
1	-	4.00	4.00	25.00	-	-	-	800/-	900/-	-	-
2	-	2.00	2.00	2.00	-	-	-	600/-	960/-	-	-
3	-	9.50	9.50	3.00	9.00	9.75	1040/-(for 1 acre)		-	-	-
					9.00	9.00	960/-(for 2 acres)				
				3.00	-	-	-	600/-	750/-	-	-
				2.00	-	-	-	600/-	750/-	-	-
				15.00	-	-	-	-	900/-(for one crop)		-
4	-	4.00	4.00	2.00	-	-	-	600/-	700/-	-	-
				15.00	-	-	-	800/-	950/-	-	-
5	-	4.50	4.50	20.00	-	-	-	600/-	800/-	-	-
				2.50	6.00	7.50	800/-	-	-	-	-
6	2	2.50	4.50	18.00	-	-	-	600/-	800/-	-	-
7	8	3.50	11.50	10.00	-	-	-	850/-	850/-	-	-
				15.00	-	-	-	800/-	850/-	-	-
				.50	7.50	7.50	800/-	-	-	-	-

8	1.60	5.00	6.60	2.50	7.50	7.50	800/-	-	-	-	-
				15.00	-	-	-			7.50	800/-
9	.65	3.00	3.65	4.00	9.00	12.00	1280/-	-	-	-	-
10	4.50	2.00	6.50	2.00	9.00	12.00	1280/-	-	-	-	-
11	3.00	2.00	5.00	2.50	9.00	9.00	960/-	-	-	-	-
				1.00	9.00	9.00	960/-				
12	8.50	8.00	16.00	15.00	-	-	-	-	-	9.00	950/-
			10.00								
13	6.50	3.50	10.00	40.00	-	-	-	-	-	9.00	900/-
				1.50	6.00	6.00	800/-	-	-	-	-
14	2.00	15.00	17.00	40.00	-	-	-	600/-	900/-	-	-
				10.00	-	9.00	960/-	-	-	-	-
				2.00	7.50	7.50	800/-	-	-	-	-
15	4.00	4.00	8.00	15.00	9.00	10.50	1120/-	-	-	-	-
				15.00	9.00	10.50	1120/-	-	-	-	-
16	2.00	3.00	5.00	15.00	7.50	9.00	960/-	-	-	-	-
				13.00	7.50	9.00	960/-	-	-	-	-
				2.00	7.50	7.50	800/-	-	-	-	-
17	3.00	3.00	6.00	12.00	-	-	-	-	-	7.50	800/-
				15.00	-	-	-	-	-	7.50	800/-
18	2.50	2.50	5.00	15.00	-	-	-	-	-	9.00	900/-
				15.00	-	-	-	-	-	7.50	800/-

Contd.\-

TABLE : 6.5 (Contd.)

1	2	3	4	5	6	7	8	9	10	11	12
19	3.00	4.00	7.00	15.00	-	-	-	-	-	9.00	950/-
				15.00	-	-	-	-	-	7.50	800/-
20	3.50	4.50	8.00	17.00	-	-	-	-	-	9.00	950/-
				13.00	-	-	-	-	-	7.50	800/-
21	3.00	4.00	7.00	15.00	-	-	-	-	-	9.00	950/-
				13.00	-	-	-	-	-	7.50	800/-
22	2.50	4.50	7.00	15.00	-	-	-	-	-	9.00	950/-
				40.00	-	-	-	-	-	9.00	950/-
23	6.00	4.00	10.00	4.00	-	-	600	600/-	900/-	-	-
24	5.00	4.00	9.00	0.80	-	-	-	600/-	800/-	-	-
				10.00	-	9.00	960/-	-	-	-	-
				15.00	-	-	-	-	950/-	-	-
25	3.00	6.00	9.00	20.00	-	-	-	720/-	800/-	-	-
				15.00	-	-	-	720/-	800/-	-	-
				13.00	-	-	-	720/-	800/-	-	-
26	3.20	4.00	7.20	40.00	-	-	-	600/-	900/-	-	-
				1.50	7.50	7.50	800/-	-	-	-	-
27	1.50	4.00	5.50	25.00	-	-	-	720/-	900/-	-	-
				15.00	9.00	10.50	1120/-	-	-	-	-

Changes in the Rate of Rent Payment

Assured canal irrigation and advent of green revolution immensely influenced the rent of land, and has significantly increased the rental value of land in the late 60s, particularly following the gains from land by intensive cultivation of HYV on a large scale. In the early 60s, when the immigrant tenants started leasing-in land, the annual rental share (for the lessor) per acre of land was 3 bags of paddy i.e. 2.25 quintals of paddy for a single crop. During a year, these immigrant tenant farmers were producing two crops thus the rent per acre used to be 4.50 quintals in a year. We have mentioned above that the rent per acre used to be still lower in the period preceding 1960, and it did not exceed Rs 33/- per acre per year. Moreover, prior to 1960 only a single crop used to be cultivated since no irrigation facilities were available in the village. But with the introduction of irrigation productivity of land has increased and gains from increased productivity have resulted in an immediate shift in the rate of rent. Every new lease is accompanied by an increase in the amount of rent.[15]

We have collected information for the year 1974 and 1975. In Table 6.5 there are 35 cases where fixed cash rents are being paid. In 15 cases rent was being paid earlier in terms of fixed amount of paddy, which has been changed to cash rent since last year (1974) and in one case the lease is a fresh one given out in 1975. In 18 out of the remaining 19 cases, the rent has been increased. The rate of increase in per acre annual rent varies from Rs 50/- to Rs 360/-. In a large number of cases the rate of increase is of the order of Rs 150/-. The enhanced rent is demanded from the same tenant if he agrees to pay the increased amount of rent, otherwise the land is leased out to a fresh tenant. Table 6.6 shows the frequency distribution of tenants paying cash rent. This includes the case of tenants where there is a shift from kind to cash rent payment.

In two out of the 21 cases, where rent is paid in fixed kind, the lease has commenced from this year. Out of the remaining 19 cases, we find in 9 cases the amount of fixed paddy rent has gone up. The rate of increase varies from 0.75 to 3 quintals of paddy over the last one year period. Among the lessors, there are 12 out of 21 who are small landowners demanding kind rent in order to meet their consumption needs.

TABLE : 6.6

Frequency Distribution of Tenants Paying Cash Rent

Rent Per Acre (In Rs)	*No. of Tenants*
700	1
750	2
800	13
850	2
900	8
950	8
960	1

Relative Resource Strength of the Lessor and the Lessee and Their Influence on Per Acre Rent

We have stated above that of the 21 cases paying fixed kind rent, in 9 cases the rental value has gone up. This apart there are two cases where the tenants are fresh ones i.e. they have started leasing in since 1975. Of these 11, only 3 are small landlords, while the remaining are big landowners. In the case of small landowners (lessors) we cannot derive any conclusion since the sample size is too small to allow generalisation. But the latter group of lessors consisting of big landowners show certain significant characteristics. These lessors have leased out land to lessees operating with holdings of less than five acres of land. In many cases they (lessees) either own no land or own a small piece of land. Therefore, leasing in is almost essential for these tenants to eke out a living. This might be largely responsible in weakening the bargaining strength of the tenants and for the rental value going up sharply in favour of lessors.

Similarly in the case of tenants paying cash rent, out of the 20 cases (where earlier cash rent used to be paid) in 19 cases tenants have been asked to pay a higher rent. Of these 19 lessees, 10 are either pure tenants or own small amount of land. Thus, the weak resource position of these tenants might be more or less responsible for the increase in the rental charges. In the remaining 9 cases, the rent has gone up but not as high as in the case of small owner-tenants or pure tenants.

In 1973-74, the demand for cash rent varied from Rs 700/- to 960/-. The landowners who were leasing out at an annual rent of Rs 700/- to 750/- were small landowners owning less than 3 acres of land whereas the lessees in these cases are better off since their operational holdings are larger, which more or less reflect the better economic status of the tenant. The lessors in this case being small land owners, possibly could not influence the rental value of the land. Consequently, the tenants seem to influence more in the determination of rent of the lease parcel. Barring a single instance in all 14 cases annual per acre rent varied from Rs 800/- to 850/-, the lessors are large landowners and therefore, enjoy a better economic status compared to their lessees. Of the 17 lessors getting annual rent of Rs 900/- to 960/- per acre all except two possess 15 or more than 15 acres of land and in these cases the economic status of the lessors is better compared to their respective lessees. During the 90s, the situation has changed. Rents have gone up and vary between Rs 1100/- to 1300/-. The small and marginal tenants have been more hard pressed compared to the better off tenants having medium size operational holdings. Similarly, big landlords have been able to extract higher amount of rent particularly when the tenant is a marginal or small farmer having very limited resources to invest in agricultural operations. Thus we may say that the relatively better resource position of the lessors has been responsible for enhancing the per acre rent of land, while lessees relatively with better resource position seem to have influenced the rent of land.

On the whole, the per acre rent has gone up. The average per acre rent for land leased out under fixed kind rent has gone up from 8.16 quintals in 1974 to 8.89 quintals per acre in 1975 and from 9 to 11 quintals per acre in the 90s. In case of fixed cash rent, the average rent has gone up from Rs 671/- to 859/- an increase of Rs 188/- over the same period while in the 1990s it has gone up to Rs 1100/- or more. The increase in the per acre rental value of land has been largely due to increase in the productivity and secondly, due to the increasing pressure on this scarce natural factor because of the influx of large number of immigrants in recent years.[16]

Changes in the Mode of Rent Payment

The increasing pressure on land in recent years not only pushed up the rental value of land but also influenced the mode of rent payment. We have already noted that cash rent was conspicuously absent in the village during the late 50s. (See Table 6.4). The lease was either given on a crop-sharing basis or on a fixed kind rent, usually the former system of lease was more in practice. But at present the cropsharing system of lease is entirely absent in the village and the lease is given only on fixed rent paid either in kind or in cash. In fact, it is the latter which is more prevalent in the village. In the sample village we have collected information from 27 out of 28 tenants, who lease in land either on fixed kind rent or on fixed cash. In all there are 56 lease units out of which 35 units are leased out on a fixed cash rent and 21 on fixed kind rent basis. Almost a similar situation prevails even during the 90s.

The gains of HYV cultivation induced the lessors to lease out land on a fixed rent basis the strategy being that such lease system will enable the lessors to capitalise the gains of HYV cultivation. There are fifteen cases where we have noted a shift from fixed kind rent system to fixed cash rent system. As we have already seen the rate of increase in the per acre rent has been more in case of fixed cash rent over the last one year period.

Lease Duration

Prior to 1960 the lessors leased out land for longer duration so that the tenant could compensate the losses of one year by a better harvest of another year.

But the situation has completely changed after the midsixties. Gains from improved methods of farming and the cultivation of HYV seem to have not only resulted in enhancing the per acre rent but, in addition, the lease durations are also shortened, increasing the insecurity of tenants. The tenant is either evicted or asked to pay the enhanced rent if he wished to continue the lease. Thus, rent of land could be increased by increasing the tenurial insecurity through reducing the lease duration.[17]

Another form of leasing land has recently developed according to which the actual lessee are shown as advancing credit to the lessor while in fact paying cash rent for leasing in land to cultivate a fixed number of crops. This device is largely adopted to defeat the impact of the land reform legislations which prohibits tenancy practices in any form. The above device makes it appear as if the land has been mortgaged for a loan to the lessee, though the loan in fact is the rent paid for the land and the 'creditor' is no one else but an actual lessee. The device thus enables the lessor to lease out the land but in the guise of a mortgage of land for a loan. In these cases of leases the duration is usually for a two crop or four crop cycle i.e. one year or for two years and rents paid are usually low since in this case the entire money rent has been advanced when the lease is decided upon. The longer is the period of lease the lower becomes the rent per acre paid for the land.

Sharing of Costs of Production

We find that all costs of production are, entirely borne by tenants. There are only a few cases where the landowners help the tenants to avail of the credit advanced through the cooperative society. In such cases the lessors do not charge any thing extra except the normal rates of interest paid to the cooperative society. This does not affect the other conditions of contract.

Lease Parcels

In this region, unlike the Irrigated Region-I (i.e. the village Lunahar in the district of Cuttack) land is not, in general, leased out in small parcels. This may be partly because of the fixed rent system of tenancy. The productive efficiency of the tenant and his resource position or viability of the operational unit seem to be of less importance, relatively speaking, under this system. Rather it appears that the system of exploitation through extracting labour services and compelling the tenant to work intensively on small parcels seems to be gradually shifting with the new technology, productivity has increased and so also input requirements. As discussed elsewhere the landlords appear how to be more interested in inducing productivity changes through, for example, fixed rents and capitalising the productivity gains mainly through increasing rents, which they do by shortening the lease periods. Thus the emphasis on leasing out in small parcels, under the earlier system of exploitation appears to have lessened.

Who Leases From Whom

Changes in the preferences for particular types of tenants were seen largely after the immigration of tenant farmers from Andhra Pradesh. Thus we have two distinct phases — the period prior to 1960 and post 1960 period in which we find sharp changes in the leasing out and leasing in pattern in the village.

Prior to 1960 land was mostly leased out on a share-cropping basis. Although, the year only one crop i.e. paddy was raised only during the *kharif* season. Irrigation facilities were not available during those days and consequently crop cultivation largely depended upon monsoon which was uncertain. Leasing in land was considered rather risky on the part of the tenant. Landlords were largely interested in leasing out to persons who could raise more output from the leased out parcel since the higher would be the produce the larger would be the rent that would accrue to the lessor. Thus, the landlords were choosy in the selection of tenants and preference was generally shown to tenants with more of manpower.

Compared to this a contrast situation has been prevailing in the post 1960 period particularly after the incoming of the Andhra migrant tenant farmers. Per acre productivity increased considerably with the introduction of irrigation, cultivation of HYV and improved technology. Consequently, the landlord's selection of tenants largely depends upon the rent that could be obtained from the tenant or in other words the land is leased out to one who offers the higher cash rent.

It is still revealing to see as to who lease in from whom. Here again, as we would see below, it is the relative resource strength of the lessor and the lessee that largely determines the lease pattern. Below, we give the matrices of lessors and lessees and the amount of land leased out or leased in respectively (See Tables 6.7 to 6.10). In order to bring out the differences in the size classes we have divided, the tenants into two different categories one, pure tenants (i.e. tenants without owned holdings and operating only the leased-in land) and the other owner-tenants. (i.e. tenants whose operational holdings includes the owned land plus the amount of land leased-in). Each category of tenants has been divided into three different size groups according to their operational holdings. The tenants operating with less than three acres of land have been categorised as small tenants, and those with operational holdings between 3 to 8 acre of land are grouped as medium class tenants and those with more than 8 acres of land have been classified as large tenant cultivators. Similar classification has been done in case of lessors but here the classification has been done on the basis of the owned holdings of the lessors. Those who own less than 3 acres of land are grouped as small lessors and lessors with more than 8 acres of owned land are categorised as big landlords.

In all, there are eleven lease units given to pure tenants out of which 6 (See Table 6.7 and 6.8) are in the medium size class, which suggests that in case of pure tenants, it is the medium class of pure tenatns who have been effective in leasing in largely from small land owners.

TABLE : 6.7

Frequency Distribution of Lease Units According to Lessee-Lessor Groups (Pure Tenants)

Operational Holding of Tenants	*Ownership Holding of Landlords*			
	0-3	*3-8*	*8+*	*Total*
0-3	1	-	-	1
3-8	3	-	3	6
8+	3	-	1	4
Total	7	-	4	11

TABLE : 6.8

Frequency Distribution of Lease Units According to Lessee-Lessor Groups (Owner-Tenants)

Operational Holding of Tenants	*Ownership Holding of Landlords*			
	0-3	*3-8*	*8+*	*Total*
0-3	-	-	-	-
3-8	6	1	23	30
8+	4	1	9	14
Total	10	2	32	44

TABLE : 6.9

Distribution of Leased Area By Lessee-Lessor Groups (Pure Tenants)

Operational Holding of Tenants (Acres)	*Ownership Holding of Landlords (Acres)*			
	0-3	*3-8*	*8+*	*Total*
0-3	2.00	-	-	2.00
3-8	5.50	-	7.00	12.50
8+	8.00	-	1.50	9.50
Total	15.50	-	8.50	24.00

TABLE : 6.10

Distribution of Leased Area By Lessee-Lessor Groups (Owner-Tenants)

Operational Holding of Tenants (Acres)	*Ownership Holding of Landlords (Acres)*			
	0-3	*3-8*	*8+*	*Total*
0-3	-	-	-	-
3-8	9.00	3.00	42.50	54.50
8+	4.80	4.00	32.20	41.00
Total	13.80	7.00	74.70	95.00

A similar lease pattern can be seen in the case of owner-tenants, too. Small owner-tenants are conspicuously absent and the medium class owner-tenants dominate the lease market (See Table 6.8), who largely lease in form big landlord only.

Considering both pure and owner-tenants together we find that the medium class lessees dominate the lease market. Out of 55 the medium class lessees (both pure and owner-cum-tenants) lease in as many as 36 lease units.

Area wise distribution of leased in and leased out land also presents a similar feature. It is again the medium class lessees in both the pure and owner tenants categories who are effective leasers-in. That the tenants with larger owned holding are not leasing in the maximum amount of land in spite of their better resource position does not contradict our statement that a tenants's resource position influences the amount of land that one can lease in. Since these tenants already own land, their operational holding would be too large to manage if they lease in considerable amount of land. Therefore, the area leased-in by the medium size class tenants both in the pure and owner-tenants categories is larger compared to the tenants in the large size and small size classes. In the 90s situation is more or less the same. We find some of the very small tenants have ceased to lease in land and have changed their profession or have left the village. This has happened in case of few Andhra immigrant tenant farmers. They had to face this because they could not pay the exorbitant rent demanded by landlords and therefore, thrown out of the lease market which is highly competitive. The complex character of the lease market hardly allows the marginal tenant farmers to continue. This is the lone reason for which the poor tenants have to quit the lease market.

Employment Situation

Introduction of irrigation facilities had a significant impact on the employment situation of the village. With the availability of irrigation facilities and the cultivation of HYV in the dry season employment opportunities have considerably increased in the area.

Prior to the mid 1960s the village Attabira was largely a monocropping area. Therefore, labour was demanded only for a few months in the year and avenues to absorb idle labour during the dry months of the year were very limited. May be it is because of this that we could find only a few labour households living in the village. Moreover as observed in the FMS, 'the major portion of the total labour force used in crop production is supplied from the farming families themselves. Some portion of the labour is also obtained in exchange or gratis. Hired labour particularly contributes not less than two-fifths of the total labour force employed in farm operations. The village *Mahajans*, *Gountias* or village Headmen carry on farming mainly with the help of hired labour. The institution of unpaid labour called *bethi begar* is in vogue and the system continues as a convention according to which each ryot provides the *Gountia* a plough and a pair of bullocks for two days during the sowing season and for two days during the harvesting time. The *Gountias* therefore, enjoy large area of land at nominal costs'.[18] The system has become almost obsolete in this region after the 60s.

Landless labour and their dependents were about one-fifth of the total population during the year 1957-60. Female labour, however, was an important component of the total labour force especially in agricultural operations like planting the seedlings, deweeding and harvesting etc.[19] But child labour (children below the age group of 14 years) was not in use in farm operations of any kind and children were engaged only in cattle grazing and more rarely in light farm operations.

To sum up, prior to 1960 employment opportunities were limited. The available labour could find, on an average, employment for 2 to 3 months in a year being unemployed during the remaining period of the year. Avenues of other alternative employment opportunities were meagre.

With the introduction of the cultivation of HYV employment opportunities has remarkably increased. Now the village Attabira is no more a monocrapping one and paddy (the major crop cultivated in the village) is grown both in the *kharif* and *rabi* seasons. Now, labour is engaged in farm operations for more than twice the time it used to be engaged earlier.

The labour households who have been living in the village could not meet the increased demand for labour when the village started growing two crops in a year. Therefore, a large number of labour households have immigrated from the neighbouring districts either temporarily (staying in the village only during the busy seasons of the year) or have settled permanently in the village. During the last one decade the number of labour households in the village has increased considerably. At present in the village Attabira, out of 817 resident families 359 are labour families. Of these a major portion are engaged in agricultural operation whereas according to the FMS during 1957-60 labour households constituted 32.37 per cent of the total number of families in the sample. This shows that the number of families engaged as labourers in the primary sector has increased considerably. Apart from the 359 labour families there are also a number of 'attached labourers' attached to different cultivating families. Above all, there is a seasonal influx of labour families who come during the busy season from the districts of Bolangir, Kalahandi and Sundargarh and also from many parts of Bilaspur district of Madhya Pradesh who are locally known as *Chattisgardi* or *Lariahs*.

Composition of Labour Force

The main components of the total labour force in the village can be classified into two broad groups — casual labourers and the permanent wage labourers. In the former category, there are the native labourers who work on daily wages, secondly, there are immigrants who have settled temporarily and work on daily wage basis and the third type of casual labourers are the immigrant labour households who come over only during the busy season and work largely on a contract basis.

The second category of permanent labourers includes the attached labourers who are one type of bonded or contract labour who work in the employer's field on annual contracts. These are called *Goti*. Another type of permanent labour is called the *Kothia* who are also employed on annual contracts. In this category, we find only the child labourers (below 14 years of age) who are employed to perform light jobs.

Casual Labourers

This includes the native labourers working mostly on daily wages. These constitutes mainly *Harijans* and *Tribals*. Some of these labour households own land. There are 7 such households (out of 13 residing permanently in the village) who possess land ranging from 0.50 acres.[20]

The second class of casual labourers are those labourers who have immigrated to the village Attabira and subsequently settled in the village. A few of them have been staying since the late 60s. Many of the immigrants came during the 70s and have managed to settle in the village. Some of these households own land in their native places and they go to their respective villages during the sowing or harvesting period. Rest of the farm operations are usually entrusted to their relations. In some cases these households lease out whatever land they own and in some cases they leave it fallow since it is not even worth while to cultivate.

The third category of casual labourers are those who come to the village only during the busy seasons in the *kharif* and the *rabi* and go back to their places of origin after the harvest of each crop. They come with their families. Some of these have land which they themselves cultivate. They usually sow the paddy and return only to harvest it. Most of these seasonal labourers hail from Chattishgarh areas of the neighbouring state Madhya Pradesh.

During the 90s, we observed that many of the cultivating households who employ the casual labourers have constructed sheds in their homestead land where these casual labourers come and stay. These cultivating households have the postal addresses of the labour households and they write to them whenever they want them to come for work. They provide them the necessary ration to cook their food during the days they work in their field. Such an arrangement ensures availability of labour whenever desired.

Most of the labour households work on contract basis though earlier they were working on daily wage basis. Contract labour here means that a piece of work is done for a fixed payment of money. The transition from employment of labour on daily wage basis to contract payment is a recent phenomenon. It has evolved particularly after the change in the mode of wage payment i.e. from kind to cash payment of wages. In addition to this, there may be another reason for which the contract system of wage payment came into existence. The immigrant labourers from Chattisgarh and Bilaspur regions were paid less wages compared to the native labourers. Therefore, they wanted to undertake jobs on piece rate basis, any by this each labourer is expected to earn more. Apparently, each labourer working on the piece rate basis would seem to earn more, but in reality they work for longer hours and put in more of labour power, because a smaller number of people take the contract of a job which otherwise requires comparatively large manpower. Presently, the contract wage system is more in vogue and field operations like transplanting, deweeding and harvesting are all being done on piece rate basis. The purpose of classifying the casual labour into three categories is to bring out the differences in the conditions of employment of each category of labour and the wages paid to them.

Permanent Labourers

Goti : These are type of attached labourers. Many of these labourers are immigrants and because of the uncertainty in employment opportunities they work as permanently attached labourers. Such form of employment assures a fixed annual income. Many of these labourers stay in the homestead land provided by the employer and are paid mostly in kind. They are not allowed to work elsewhere during the contract period. These attached labourers are employed mostly in the agricultural operations in the field. Sometimes they are asked also to work during night and the nature of work ranges from household work to field operations.

Similar to the *goties* there is another kind of labourers who work on cash wages paid on monthly basis. These labourers are not employed all through the year but are enaged for about 8 to 9 month in a year. During the contract period they are to abide by conditions similar to that of the *goties*. This class of casual labourers is of recent origin.

Kothia

The second category of attached labourers are called the *Kothia*. The *Kothia* labourers are mostly children employed for cattle grazing and for light farm operations, sometimes to assist ploughing the field, and sometimes in household activities. Usually these *Kothia* labourers stay in the employer's house all day and night and have food three times during the day in the employer's house.

Employment of Labour

It may be noticed from our observations that both owner cultivators and tenant farmers employ casual as well as permanent labourers. Demand for labourers was not so intense in the pre-irrigation period when family labour in many cases was sufficient to meet the needs. But the cultivation of paddy in both the *kharif* and the *rabi* seasons generated demand for more labour force.

Many of the owner cultivators do not actively participate in farm operations. Quite a number of them do only supervisory work even though self-cultivation has been resorted to seriously by some owner-cultivators after the introduction of irrigation and cultivation of HYV.[21] Out of the 45 owner-cultivators in our sample 29 are actively engaged in cultivation while 16 do not actively participate in field operations except doing supervisory work. In all cases except 7 we do not find owner-cultivators engaging their female family members in active farm operations, because this is considered derogatory for one's family status. Therefore, all the owner-cultivators including the ones engaging their family labour in actual process of cultivation hire labour for some farm operations.

In some cases, we note that the owner-cultivators with small operational holding of below 2 acres hire out labour during the days when they are not engaged in their own field. But it is difficult to calculate the number of days they work outside their own farm since they work off and on. But in no case they go out to work if their own farm requires their labour.

In all, the tenant cultivating households we notice that one or two male members of the family actively participate in the process of cultivation. There are only 10 tenant cultivating families (out of 27) who use female labour of their own families. Participation by female members is considered to be socially unacceptable. This is more particularly so in the case of the Andhra immigrant tenants. Of the 27 tenant families 19 have employed attached labourers. In many cases this becomes an essential supplement to the family labour.

Preference for Different Types of Labours

We note certain specific preferences arising in the case of employment of labour. As we have stated earlier, labour enaged on contract basis i.e. contract for piece rate work, is a recent phenomenon. The employment of labour on contract basis is seen to have become increasingly popular. Of the 45 owner-cultivators covered our sample, 34 prefer to engage labour on contract basis where as only 9 prefer to enage labour daily wage basis and 2 owner-cultivators show their indifference between either category of wage labour. Higher demand for contract labour may be largely due to the fact that the work is done faster. Especially, during the planting of seedling sould be executed with speed, for example they say that work should be executed with speed, for example the plantation of seedling should be done quickly since the earlier it is done the less is the possibility of a pest attack and the plants grow sufficiently before the actual breeding season of the pests (Gall Midge) starts. This is particularly so during the *kharif* season. Moreover, with the supervision of the employer the work is not only done faster but better too. It is also noticed that contract labour works out to be cheaper than employing labour on daily wages for any specific job.

So far as the tenant cultivators are concerned we find a similar inclination towards employment of contract labour. Out of the 27 tenants, contract labour is preferred by 21 and the remaining 6 prefer to employ labour on daily wages. In the latter case, the preference for daily wage earners may be due to the fact these farmers have family labour as well as attached labourers who work in the field. Therefore, they employ casual labour on daily wage basis merely to supplement the already available labour on the farm.

A difference is also noticed in the demand for immigrant and local labourers. Here, we include in the former group of immigrant labour the labourers who immigrate only during the busy season especially the 'Chattisgarhi' labourers from Bilaspur. Opinions with regard to the efficiency of either categories of labour widely differ. While some consider the Chatisgarhi labour to be more efficient, others report that the local labourers are more skilled. From our observations, we notice that 19 out of 45 owner-cultivators actually prefer immigrant labourers and only 4 prefer the local agricultural labourers where as the remaining 22 are indifferent and could not give any particular preference. Similarly in the case of tenant farmers, there is greater demand for immigrant labourers. Of the 27 tenant farmers 15 prefer immigrant farm labourers while only 2 prefer local labourers. The remaining 10 tenant farmers do not show any particular preference and remain indifferent.

Apart from employing casual labourers many of the owner cultivators have employed attached labourers, of the 45 , 32 self-cultivating families have attached labourers. The number of attached labourers and the type of attached labourers vary depending upon the work load of field operation.

Wage Rates

Farm labourers are employed either on casual or on permanent basis. Earlier we stated that all these labourers are not from Attabira village originally. The local labouorers constitute only a small proportion of the total labour force engaged in farm operations. A large proportion of the total labour have immigrated and have settled down in the village during the last one decade. The influx of the farm labourers to the village has a great impact on the wage rates, which have changed considerably. We find the wage rate to be varying gradually in recent years. Moreover, the striking change that we notice in the recent period is the introduction of contract wage system.

Prior to the introduction of irrigation and the cultivation of the HYV, i.e. prior to 1960s, we notice the wage rates to be very low, and wages were largely paid in kind. Table 6.11 shows the average wages paid during the years in the late 50s. All except child labourers were engaged for 8 hours. The children were either employed to do light farm work or to look after the cattle. The average wages given in the table for different years indicate an increasing trend in wage rate for all men, women and children.[22]

The present wage rates do show that wage rates have changed over considerably in the late 60s. A sharp change was noticed in 1969 when the HYV paddy began to be cultivated on a large scale during the *rabi* season.

Table 6.12 gives the frequency distribution of male and female labourers according to the wages rates. So far as the immigrant labour households are concerned we have divided them into two categories: those who have stayed in the village for more than 3 years have been included in the category of local labourers since they preseumably enjoy a better bargaining power than those who have stayed for a shorter period. Therefore, the latter category of labourers i.e. those who have stayed for a period of less than 3 years have been included in the category of immigrants.

It is explicit from the table that the wage rate for female labour is lower than the wage paid to the adult male labourers, except in a single case of immigrant labourer who gets Rs 2.50 as daily wage. There are 22 female labourers getting Rs. 2.50 and there are 3 who get Rs 2/- as daily wage whereas there is not a single case where a female labourer gets Rs 3.50 which is the mode value of wage rate paid to male labourers.

TABLE : 6.11*

Average Daily Wage Rates of Agricultural Labourer During 1957-60

Year	*Male*		*Female*		*Child*	
	Cash	*Kind*	*Cash*	*Kind*	*Cash*	*Kind*
1957-58	0.89	0.91	0.68	0.69	0.58	0.54
1958-59	0.93	0.92	0.69	0.74	0.69	0.67
1959-60	0.87	0.96	0.89	0.73	-	0.75
Average	0.92	0.93	0.72	0.71	0.64	0.61

* Source: *F.M.S.*, (Sambalpur District), 1960. op.cit. p.33.

TABLE : 6.12

Frequency Distribution of Male and Female Labourers (Both Immigrants and Local) According to Wage Received in 1975

Type of Labour	*Male*			*Female*			*Total*
	Rs 2.50	*Rs 3.00*	*Rs 3.50*	*Rs 2.50*	*Rs 3.00*	*Rs 3.50*	-
Local*	-	5	22	11	17	-	55
Immigrants**	1	17	4	12	2	Nil	36

* Local labourers include here also the labour households who have settled in the village for more than three years.

** Immigrant labourers include those who come only during the peak seasons, and also those who have immigrated to the village and settled for less than a period of three years.

The difference in the wage rates paid to the local and immigrant labourers can be clearly seen from the Table 6.13. While at low wage rates frequency of immigrant labourers is more than that of the local labourers, at higher wage rate we find frequency of immigrant labourers dwindling whereas that of the local labourers increase. A similar trend is also noticeable in the case of female labourers (See Table 6.13). We also find that there are some labourers who work at lower wages in a creditor's field as a form of part repayment for a loan. Generally, in such cases the wages paid are lower than the market wage rate.

Thus in general, we may infer that the local labourers get higher wages compared to the immigrants because of their greater bargaining power. We have noted in the 90s, while doing the resurvey, that most agricultural operations are done on contract basis. The immigrant labourers are hard working and are preferred to the native labourers. The wage paid on contract has gone up but not significantly as reported by the labourers.

Mode of Wage Payments

Prior to 1960, wages were paid mostly in kind, generally, in terms of paddy. Wages paid in terms of cash were negligible.[23] Such a system of kind payment continued till 1969, when wage rates gradually changed and labourers were paid in terms of cash. Particularly since 1971-72 wages are being paid entirely in terms of cash.

Unlike casual labourers who are paid in cash, the attached labourers are mostly paid in kind. The annual wages and the monthly maintenance expenses are all paid in kind mainly in terms of paddy. Of course, there is one class of attached labourers who are paid in terms of money. These are the labourers who work on monthly wages of Rs 90/- and work with the employer for 7 to 8 months in a year.

Attached Labourers

We have indicated earlier the different forms of attached labourers. Here we will discuss only the conditions of employment and the reasons if any for their becoming attached labourers.

There are 37 families where the heads of the families are attach labourers. In many cases the family consists of some more members who also work as attached labourers. In many of these households, there are child labourers working as *Kothia* (i.e. one type of attached labourer), already mentioned.

Earlier Status of Attached Labourers

We have covered in our survey 13 out of 36 attached labour families in Attabira, 5 of these have been attached labourers over many years while three were formerly (i.e. prior to 1964) daily wage earners; another 3 were cultivating their own land, but because of the break up of joint family household 2 have left self-cultivation. In one of the two households the labourer lost the land to other members of the family while in the other two cases, his share of the landed property became an uneconomic unit and had to be leased out. The rest two households who were earlier leasing in land have abandoned the practice because of increasing rents and have become attached labourers.

Out of the 13 attached labour households 9 possessed land out of which only 5 are even now holding land. In other cases either thc land has been sold out or lost to money lenders for non-repayment of the loan. Out of the 5 cases who possess land, in two cases, the land owned is not cultivable and in one case the unit of the land is uneconomical for cultivation. Consequently these have been leased out to their kith and kin who stay in their villages.

Employment Conditions

All these attached labourers are employed on an annual contract basis at the beginning of each agricultural year. According to the contract most of them receive their wages in kind, usually in terms of paddy.

We have referred earlier to three different kinds of attached labourers. *Goties* are usually paid in kind. Annually, they are paid a lump sum of 5.5 to 7.5 quintals of paddy (depending upon the efficiency of individual attached labourers) usually paid at the end of February every year. This apart in each case they are paid a maintenance allowance. They are also given a pair of *dhoties* and a *gamchha* and a *chadar* annually. But in this case the payment is more of a convention than a part of contract and the practice is not uniform. There are two cases where one is given only one *dhoti* while the other one has not been given anything. Similarly 8 of the 13 attached labourers get a *gamchha* and a *chadar* each while others do not get anything. Above all some of these *goties* are given a small parcel of homestead land where they build their huts to live in. Some of the employers supply materials to raise such huts. Some of the attached labourers also get small parcels of land, measuring about 20 to 25 cents, from their employer. The total produce raised from this plot of land belongs to the labourer while all costs of cultivation is borne by the employer. All these, the labourer gets in addition to the wages.

The second category of attached labourers who are employed are paid Rs 90/- per month. But they are not employer on annual contracts. They perform tasks similar to those performed by *goties*.

The third category of attached labourers, the *kothias*, are mostly engaged in light farm work and cattle grazing and household work etc. These *kothias* are paid about 5 quintals of paddy (the amount varies according to one's efficiency) per annum and given food three times a day through out the year.

Other Conditions of Employment of Attached Labourers

All these different kinds of labourers are not allowed any kind of leave except on festive occasions like the *rath yatra* or in cases of physical ailment and marriage of the labourer himself. Leave of this sort is restricted to 4 to 5 days in a year. During this leave sometimes the employer demands for substitutes. Thus these attached labourers are required to work through out their period of employment. In some cases (2 out of the 13 attached labour households in our sample) they are allowed leave for 4 to 6 days in a year. If the leave exceeds this period they are required to provide a substitute or forgo the wages for that period of absence. In any case, they cannot remain absent for long period.

Usually, these attached labourers are required to work

for eight hours a day. But some times especially during the peak periods they are asked to work for more than the stipulated time for which no extra payment is made. For example, some attached labourers are asked to watch the field, to control the water supply during the night or to attend to some household work. During peak period, they work continuously over 10 hours and are not paid additional wages. The *kothias*, however, work for longer hours and this is largely because of the nature of job (like tending cattle) that varies from that of the *goties*.

All these various kinds of attached labourers however, are not allowed to work elsewhere. The employers keep them engaged through out the year.

Attached labourers are economically better off compared to the daily wage earners because employment and hence subsistence is assured all through the year. The duration as well as the nature of work varies considerably between the two categories of labour. While the daily wage earner has the 'freedom' of movement and 'choice of work' the attached labourers have to work according to the desires of their employers.

To conclude, we have noted the transition that has taken place in the village Attabira between 1964 to 1975 and again in the 1990s. The total population, particularly those engaged in the agricultural sector have increased giving rise to increased demand for land. There is a large immigration of tenant farmers from the neighbouting districts and particularly from Andhra. The increased demand for land conjointly with increased per acre productivity have been largely responsible for enhancing the rental value of land. What is significant is that crop-sharing tenancy has completely given way to fixed rent system of lease paid either in kind or cash and fixed cash rent paid in advance. In fact it is the latter which is more prevalent in the village. In order to appropriate the gains of green revolution the landlords, particularly the large landowners, have not only increased the per acre rent but also have shortened the lease duration, increasing conspicuously the tenurial insecurity.

Though under a fixed rent lease system it is generally presumed that leasing in and leasing out of land would be largely determined by the per acre rent, it is still interesting to note how the relative resource strength influences the lease pattern. The tenants operating with medium size holdings appear to be more prominent both numerically and area wise.

Employment opportunities have increased with adoption of HYV and multiple cropping. We find a large influx of labour families, some settling in the village and some immigrating during the peak seasons only. Preference for different type of labourers are distinctly evident in the village. While a few prefer to employ the local labourers, a large number of cultivators (both tenant and owner cultivators) seem to prefer the immigrant labourers since the latter group of labourers are considered to be more efficient. The wage rates have gone up in the recent years and wages are no more being paid in kind. A system of contract payment on piece rate basis is increasingly in vogue in the recent years.

REFERENCES

1. As the name indicates it is the village of which the early settlers were the inferior descendants of the *Gountia* families. These descendants were asked to settle in this village since they picked up disputes with the *Gountia* family. They were thus given inferior quality of land with low fertility called the *Tikra* land, since then this village has been recognised as Beiman Tikra.
2. Tehsil Reports for the Village Attabira, 1975.
3. Land value was very low when irrigation was not provided to the area and it remained so even in the early days after the introduction of irrigation. This attracted many peasant farmers of Andhra to immigrate to the district of Sambalpur. In fact a large number of Andhra immigrant farmers are seen to have settled in many village of the districts some owning more than 60 acres of land and having mechanised farming. In fact the influx of tenant farmers is not only confined to this village alone and we notice them to have spread over the different parts of

Sambalpur districts. The immigration of these cultivators was noticeable in the 60s. Even now we find some to be still coming though the intensity has slowed down.

4. Cultivation of HYV in the *kharif* season has started the introduction of a new variety of seed namely 'Jagannath' which is supposed to be pest resistant.
5. *Farm Management Studies* (FMS), Sambalpur District, op. cit. p.81.
6. Ibid. p. 83.
7. Ibid. pp. 83-84.
8. Ibid. pp. 83-85.
9. Ibid. p. 86.
10. Here we have worked out the per acre demand for labour to avoid the complication of computing the cost of family labour. Even then supervisory work done by the landholder and the occasional input of family labour cannot be computed.
11. Also see Krishna Bharadwaj 'Notes on Farm Size and Productivity' *Economic and Political Weekly*, Review of Agricultural (March 30, 1974); A.K. Bagchi, 'Some implication of unemployment in rural areas', *Economic and Political Weekly* (Special Number August, 1973) pp. 1501-1510.
12. FMS op. cit. p.89
13. Krishna Bharadwaj — *Production Conditions in Indian Agriculture* op. cit. p.53.
14. '... the advent of new technology confronts the small owner-cum-tenants cultivators with the bleak prospect not only of increasing economic disparity, but also of an agonising change from security in the midst of poverty to growing insecurity along with poverty.' F.R. Frankel. *India's Green Revolution Economic Gains and Costs*, Oxford University Press, 1971, p. 197.
15. 'Certainly the landowners do not hesitate to raise the rentals in line with appreciating land values and /or evicting tenant having long standing cultivating possession of the land.' Frankel, Ibid, p. 197.
16. As population and production increased the landowners could extract higher rent without paying higher taxes... the rent receiving interest grew parasitically without contributing to increased production... the cultivator had to pay what ever rent was exacted, under penalty of eviction. Dooner Warainer — *Land*

Reforms in Principle and Practice (Claredon Press, Oxford, 1969), p. 158. see also p.148.

17. Krishna Bharadwaj, *Production conditions in Indian Agriculture* op. cit. p.53.
18. FMS, Sambalpur District, Op. cit. p.32.
19. Ibid-p.32.
20. This apart there are some *Harijans* who have occupied by force some government land and are cultivating since 1975.
21. FMS, Sambalpur District, op. cit. pp. 32-33.
22. FMS, Sambalpur District, op. cit. p.33.
23. FMS, Sambalpur District, op. cit. p. 32.

7
SUMMARY AND CONCLUSION

This study looks into some aspects of tenurial conditions in Orissa. Tenurial condition in the State acquired complexity because Orissa was under different political administration, which influenced the evolution of tenurial relations. The landlord-tenant relationship, quite often than not, is characterised by the exploitation of tenatns who depend largely on leasing in land to eke out a living. The situation is all the more worse because agriculture is the major source of living in rural Orissa. Consequently, rackrenting, eviction and exploitation of the tenantry has been rampant in the State over many decades. The evils of tenurial systems are so deep rooted that the various land legislations during the post-independence period more or less failed to achieve any improvement in the situation. The old patterns of feudal landlordism appears to be still persisting in many villages of Orissa. We have analysed the production relationship that exists in agriculture at two different points of time — 1974-75 and 1990 and we could see that the situation has worsened. The exploitative grip of the landlords has been further strengthened because the tenants do not have any viable alternative source of livelihood. The intricacies of the lease market and factor market have adversely affected the tenants. Any change in the infrastructure which has helped in increasing productivity in agriculture has been successfully capitalised by the landlords.

Analytical studies on various aspects of tenancy available as yet appear to be inadequate as most of them are based on stylised situations using restrictive information. To understand, the functioning of the lease market and the landlord-tenant relationship under any land tenure system it is essential to study the respective socio-economic status of lessors and lessees participating in the lease market. We have made an attempt to analyse the tenurial relation through enquiring into questions like 'who leases from whom'. This provides a basis for the study of not only the terms and conditions of the lease but also the various factors responsible for leasing in and leasing out and to look at forces of change in the prevailing situation. These aspects have been dealt with extensively where we stress the inter-mixed characteristics (monopolistic and monoposonistic) of the landlease market. Given a skewed distribution of ownership of land there exists a class of landowners, who appears to dominate the supply side in the lease market. Simultaneously, we find a large mass of land hungry tenants eager to lease in land to raise their own subsistence. But all tenants do not seem to have equal access to the lessors and the emerging land lease pattern in the different villages under study shows that lessees with some amount (but not substantial) of owned land or lessees who have some amount of land already leased in appear to be most effective. The mere desire is not enough to acquire leases. There are various considerations that influence the availability of land to be leased out to those who are interested in leasing in. The landless though are very keen to lease in are less favoured by landlord because they lack investible resources. The big tenants who also desire to lease in are not always preferred by lessors presumably because such tenants may neglect the leased in land. Very small and small tenants appear to be more amenable to exploitation by lessors who dominate the supply side. In the absence of alternative source of earning the small tenants tend to put in the maximum amount of labour power to increase the total produce on the leased in parcel. This may explain why landlords are inclined to leasing out to tenants either with a small amount of owned land or pure tenants with some amount of land leased in, resulting in the numerical predominance of tenants operating with small and medium size holdings.

It has also been observed that it is not the big landowners who are interested to lease out. We also find that even marginal or very small landowners who leased out land to be cultivated by tenant farmers. But the considerations of leasing out by the big landowners and also by small or marginal landowners appear to be different. While the big landowners lease out with a motive to earn rent the small landowners do it under distress, because they cannot undertake self-cultivation for lack of labour and non-labour resources.

Most of the landlords show a preference to leae out land in small parcels. Such a preference exists particularly in the Irrigated Region I whereas in Irrigated Region II the lease parcels are generally given in large sizes. While in the former case the main consideration is that small operational holding would induce the tenant to produce more, in the latter case, since the leases are given on fixed rents the land is leased out to one who offers the highest rent. In the unirrigated areas the big landlords lease out in somewhat bigger parcels presumably because, with land being unirrigated, the 'economic' unit may be somewhat larger than in the case of irrigated land. In the tribal areas, the big landowners generally prefer to lease out in small parcels. In all these cases, the lessors appears to be more concerned over the amount of rent that would accrue to them and availing of the other advantages that accompany the lease.

The initial resource position not only influences the lease pattern but also to some extent the considerations for leasing in and leasing out. While we find many landlords lease out because of caste inhibitions or because they are ‘traditional landlords’, many landlords also lease out under distress conditions. There are also landowners, particularly the big landowners in the irrigated areas, who lease out because they find it lucrative to do so.

The initial resource position largely determines the terms and conditions. We focus particularly on the terms and conditions of lease. Depending upon the social and agro-economic conditions prevailing in the different areas the tenurial patterns and conditions differ. We find while the small tenants are subjected to more exploitative situations particularly when they are leasing in from large landowners, the bigger tenants appear to enjoy a relatively favourable bargaining power. It is revealing to note the situation when a landlord has multiple tenants with varying resource positions. Tenants with relatively inferior economic status appear to have adverse lease terms whereas big tenants seem to enjoy a relatively better bargaining status. Thus even under identical tenurial systems we find different lease terms and conditions to co-exist.

Apart from land rent the tenant farmers particularly the socially and economically weaker ones seen to be rendering free or underpaid labour services to the lessor who is usually a big landowner. Occasional 'gifts' are also offered to such landowners to keep them in good humour so that the lease is not discontinued. A typical feudal characteristic appear to exist even now in the rural economy of Orissa. The tenants are under duress and are subjected to the different forms of exploitation because they do not have any other alternative source to eke out a living.

We also find situations where the feudal mode has given way and is replaced by a sort of capitalist mode of production. This transitional phase, we could say, a semi-feudal or a precapitalist mode production prevailing in the backward agrarian economy of rural Orissa. In some cases, where the landlords stipulate production of particular crop, namely cash crop, where the yield rate is expected to be more, landlords advance credit to the poor tenants because otherwise production of such crops is highly unlikely. The tenant under distress has to accept such credit largely to satisfy the desire of the landlrod and secondly he also expects higher returns from the leased in land parcels which may increase his income. Even if this gain is only marginal this induces him to accept the credit. Thus, the lessors are successful in capitalising the gains of increased productivity and exploiting the poor tenants through land and lending.

Situation is still worse in case where the lessor combines the functions of usury and landownership. In most of the villages particularly in the tribal belts or in villages producing cash crop we have noted that the putting out system i.e. advancing credit either to cultivate the stipulated crop or to satisfy consumption needs, plays an important role in deciding the production relations that exist today in rural Orissa.

The modern inputs whether canal irrigation or use of fertiliser etc. have increased the total output or per acre productivity. But it appears that these gains have not mitigated the sufferings of the poor tenant farmers but has rather, resulted in increasing their miseries. The difference in income has widened, the poor has become poorer and is unable to satisfy the basic minimum essential for their survival. The complexities existing in the lease market have almost forced them to quit and seek other sources of livelihood either in the labour market or elsewhere.

In Phulbani district largely inhabited by tribal population we have noted similar occurrences where a shopowner has a large number of small tenants whom he expects to buy grocery etc. from his small shop. He sells them on credit and poor tenants being hardpressed had to buy their requirements from him. Since they buy the commodities on credit their poverty get perpetuated. Abysimal poverty becomes chronic and the growing indebtedness put all marginal tenant-cultivators in a precarious situation.

We have made an indepth study of Attabira village where, we note that tenurial practices have changed with the changing agro-economic conditions. In the village Attabira, with the adoption of HYV paddy cultivation landlords have resorted to different tenurial arrangements in order to retain their exploitative hold. A transition from share-cropping tenancy to fixed rent lease, paid mostly in cash and in advance is again a recent phenomenon. We have analysed these changes that have taken place in this village regard to the parties involved in the lease, terms and conditions of lease and the employment situation (with respect to both the extent as well as terms of employment) for different categories of labourers with a gap of more than one and half decades and the study shows that situation has further worsened i.e., the tenants are still subjected to the exploitative hold of the landlords and have remote chances of coming out of the trap.

INDEX